02-02-2021

Linda F Rebon

Moments On The Mount

MOMENTS ON THE MOUNT:

A SERIES OF

DEVOTIONAL MEDITATIONS.

BY

REV. GEORGE MATHESON, M.A., D.D.

MINISTER OF THE PARISH OF INNELLAN.

Second Edition.

NEW YORK:

A. C. ARMSTRONG & SON, 51 EAST 10TH ST.

PREFACE.

THERE are two motives which have influenced us in the production of this little book. We have sought, on the one hand, to supply aids to devotion either for the use of the family or of the individual, and on the other, to furnish points of suggestion to the student who is a prospective preacher. Perhaps it may be thought that these two aims are incongruous, and it would be too much to hope that in both we have succeeded; yet devotion is not the absence of thought, and thought is not necessarily the absence of devotion. At all events, the presence in the mind of two so reactionary aims may have had the beneficial result of preserving these meditations either from the fault of too much abstractness or from the sin of too little depth.

G M.

MANSE, INNELLAN, 1884.

CONTENTS.

MOMENTS ON THE MOUNT.

———

I.

QUIET MOMENTS.

"And they heard the voice of the Lord God walking in the garden in the cool of the day."—GEN. iii. 8.

IT is only in the cool of the day that I can hear Thy footsteps, O my God. Thou art ever walking in the garden. Thy presence is abroad everywhere and always; but it is not everywhere nor always that I can hear Thee passing by. The burden and heat of the day are too strong for me. The struggles of life excite me, the ambitions of life perturb me, the glitter of life dazzles me; it is all thunder and earthquake and fire. But when I myself am still I catch Thy still small voice, and then I know that Thou art God. Thy peace can only speak to my peacefulness, Thy **rest can** only be audible to my **calm**; the harmony of Thy tread cannot be heard by the discord of my soul. Therefore, betimes I would be alone with Thee, away from the heat and the battle. I would feel the cool breath of Thy Spirit, **that** I may be refreshed once more for the strife. I would be fanned by the breezes of heaven, that I may resume the dusty road and the dolorous way. Not to avoid them do I come to Thee, but that I may be able more perfectly to bear them. Let me hear Thy voice in the garden in the cool of the day.

II.

UNSELFISH MOMENTS.

"And the Lord turned the captivity of Job when he prayed for his friends."—JOB xlii. 10.

IT is only in moments of unselfishness that I am free. The iron chain that binds me is the thought of myself and of my own calamities; if I could but be liberated from that, my captivity would be turned in an hour. If, under the shadow of the cloud, I could but remember that the shadow of the same cloud hovers over my brother-man, the vision of his shadow would destroy mine. In the moment of prayer for him my burden would fall from me. I would seek it, and lo! it would not be found; it would be as if it had not been. O Thou Divine Spirit of self-forgetfulness, Spirit of Christ, Spirit of the Cross, it is in Thee alone that I can find this freedom. Liberate me from myself, and instead of the iron chain, give me a chain of gold. It is not the chain that lowers me, it is the material of which it is made; it is not the sorrow that makes me a captive, it is the centring of the sorrow round my own life. Help me to take up the burdens of others. Help me to know what it is to have rest in bearing an additional yoke, Thy yoke, the yoke of humanity. Help me to feel what it is to have peace in carrying a new care, Thy care, the care of universal love. Help me to learn what it is to be transfigured in the prayer for others; to have the countenance shining as the light, and the raiment white and glistering

My fetters shall be wings of sympathy whereby I shall pass into the heart of the world, and when I have reached the heart of the world the fetters shall fall ; my captivity shall be turned back when I have prayed for my captive friends.

III.

THE BRIGHT LIGHT IN THE CLOUDS.

"*And now men see not the bright light which is in the clouds.*"—JOB xxxvii. 21.

MY soul, the greatest truth about thee is that which thou hast not learned—the secret of thine own joy, the source of the light that is in thee. Thou art seeking thy light in the dispersion of the cloud, and all the time Thy light is *in* the cloud. Thou art like the old patriarch of Uz. Thou art asking God for an explanation of thy darkness, and thou art expecting an answer from all quarters but one —the darkness itself. Yet it is there, and nowhere else, that the secret lies. Thy cloud is thy fire-chariot; thy trial is thy triumph.

The best gift of divine love to thee has been thy pain; it has taught thee what is the difference between being virtuous and being innocent. Thou hast been self-deceived, O my soul. Thou hast been down in the valley of the shadow, and thou hast been looking up to the calm heavens to find thy God. The calm heavens have not answered thee, and thou hast said, " Verily Thou art a God that hidest Thyself." Yet all the time thy God has been beside thee in the valley, a sharer in the shadow of thy life. Thou hast been looking too far to find Him; thou has cried to the heavens when He was at the very door. He was speaking in the voices that seemed to deny His presence; He was manifested in the shades that appeared to veil His form. He came to thee in the night, that His glory might be concealed. He came to thee unaccompanied and unadorned, that He might know whether He were loved for Himself alone. The night under which thou hast murmured has been hiding in its folds a wondrous treasure—the very presence of the King of kings; wherefore didst thou not see the bright light in the cloud?

IV.

THE MYSTERY OF GOD'S LEADING.

"God led them not through the way of the land of the Philistines, although that was near . . . but God led the people about through the way of the wilderness."—
Exod. xiii. 17–18.

WHY is it that I am not suffered to come to Thee by the near way? wherefore am I forced to seek the promised land through the longest road—the road of the wilderness? There are times when I almost seemed to have reached Thee at a bound. There are flashes of thought in which I appear to have escaped the wilderness and to have entered already into Thy rest. I am caught up to meet Thee in the air, and the world fades away in the far distance, and I am alone with Thyself. But the rapture and the solitude are short-lived. The world returns again with double power, and a cloud falls over the transfiguration glory; and at the very moment when I am saying, "Methinks it is good to be here," a voice whispers in my ear, " Go back, and take the journey through the wilderness."

My soul, thou must not murmur at that message ; it is a message of love to thee, and a message of love to the wilderness. Thou hast need of the wilderness, and the wilderness has need of thee. There are thorns in the desert which must be gathered ere she can rejoice and blossom as the rose, and the gathering of her thorns shall be the gathering of flowers to thee. Thou canst not do without the thorn. To be caught up to meet thy Lord in the air would be too much exaltation ; it would lift thee above the sympathies of the toiling crowd. Better to meet thy Lord in the wilderness than in the air. Thou wilt find him travelling by the long road—the road of Gethsemane and Calvary. Join thyself to the journey of the Son of man. Help Him to carry His burden of human care over the wastes of time. Enter into fellowship with that cross of His which was the pain of seeing pain, and verily love shall make the long road short ; thy feet shall be as the feet of the roe ; the crooked shall be made straight,

Need of the wilderness?

and the rough places shall be made plain; for the glory of the Lord shall be revealed, and the glory of the Lord is love.

V.

THE TROUBLE BROUGHT BY CHRIST.

" When Herod the king had heard these things, he was troubled."—MATT. ii. 3.

THERE were four kingdoms congregated at the Christian dawn—the kingdom of nature, the kingdom of knowledge, the kingdom of worldliness, and the kingdom of unworldliness. The kingdom of nature came in a star, the kingdom of knowledge in the Magi, the kingdom of worldliness in Herod, and the kingdom of unworldliness in the child-Christ. Only one of the kingdoms was troubled by the child. Nature did not fear Him, knowledge did not shun Him; Herod alone trembled at His coming.

My soul, art thou afraid of the coming of Christ into thy life? Dost thou fear that He will narrow thee? Nay, but He will narrow that which narrows thee. He will not destroy thy love of nature, for He is the crown of nature. He will not dispute thy right to knowledge, for He is the end of knowledge; but He will expel from thy heart the Herod that imprisons thee. He will deny the power of Herod to make thee happy, and He will prove His denial even by thy pain. Wouldst thou rather be without that pain? Hast thou forgotten the pool of Bethesda? An angel came down to trouble the waters, and then the waters were powerful. Thou, too, shalt be powerful after thou hast been troubled. Thinkest thou that the stillness of primeval chaos was a calm? There was no calm till the Spirit moved. Only when the face of the waters is ruffled by the breath of the life Divine is the mandate truly heard, "Let there be light."

VL

GOD'S SYMPATHETIC KNOWLEDGE.

" The Lord knoweth the way of the righteous."—
Ps. i. 6.

Does He not know all things? Why limit thus the range of His omniscience? Is there anything that can be hid from the search of His piercing gaze? Is not the way of the wicked also known to Him?—known so well that He has travelled over the far country to seek and to save that which was lost. Yes; but there is a sense in which He only knows the good. His eyes behold, His eyelids try all that *belongs* to the eye; but there is a knowledge which belongs not to the eye but to the heart, the knowledge which men call sympathy. Hundreds know me as a man, but only my child knows me as a father. Even so the heavenly Father has a special knowledge of His child. His knowledge is his nearness; it is the attraction of a kindred sympathy, the gravitation of love. He looks into the glass of our humanity and He beholds there, in miniature, the brightness of His own glory, the express image of His own person, the Christ that is to be, and when He sees it, He rejoices with an exceeding great joy.

My soul, wilt thou fulfil this joy of thy Father's heart? He waits to behold in thee the impress of His own likeness. He sits as a refiner of silver till He sees in thee the reflection of His own image, and when He sees His image reflected He knows that the refining is complete. Wilt thou grant Him the joy of that knowledge? Wilt thou let Him behold a Christ in thee—Himself in thee? Wilt thou let Him feel that there is a heart in sympathy with His heart, a life in unison with His life, a will in harmony with His will? Then thou shalt have the joy of all joys—the joy of making glad the heart of God. Communion is dear to the spirit of the heavenly Father; for the spirit of the Father is love, and love seeketh not her own. It cannot rest in aught but the vision of its object; it must speak, and it must be answered again; it must know even as it is known.

VII.

INTERRUPTED COMMUNION.

"Go, get thee down ; for thy people, which thou broughtest out of the land of Egypt, have corrupted themselves."— EXOD. xxxii. 7.

"Go, get thee down ;" it was surely a hard, an unlikely mandate. Was it not a command to go forth from the secret of God's pavilion, from the Mount of Divine vision and Divine communion into the vision of things that were not Divine, into communion with things that were not holy ? You and I have been forced at times to feel what Moses felt. We have had moments of rapture, in which we have been allowed to stand on the very top of the mountain and to see, as it were, the face of God unveiled—moments when His countenance was radiant as the light and His raiment dazzling as the sunlit snow. But presently a cloud has fallen over the vision and the glory has vanished from the scene. The rapture is turned into coldness, and the mountain sinks into a common plain, filled with the concourse of the multitude, and echoing with the cries of human struggle; a voice has sounded in mine ear and said, " Go, get thee down."

Yes, my soul, and has it not brought to thine ear the reason of its sounding? Why has it commanded thee to quit the glorious mountain for the common plain? It is because it *is* a common plain. It is because on that plain there is a concourse of living beings who are unfit for the glorious mountain. They have no vision from a height, and therefore they are oppressed by life's labour and its ladenness. They want some one to heal them, some one to lift them, some one to inspire them with the breath of a presence that has dwelt aloft. Thou mayest be that presence. If thou hast gazed on the face of God, thou hast a mesmeric passport into the heart of thy brother man. He shall lift up his eyes unto the hills, whence cometh *thine* aid; make no tarrying to go down, O my soul.

VIII.

THE VISION OF THE STAR.

" When they had heard the king, they departed ; and, lo,
the star, which they saw in the east, went before them."
—MATT. ii. 9.

WHERE had the star been while they tarried
in the city of Herod ? Had it ceased to shine
in the sky ? Had it been extinguished when
it had led them to the palace of the great
king ? Nay, it was still there, but they had
lost sight of it; it was hidden by the streets
and buildings of the world. The wise men
had entered into an uncongenial atmosphere,
into a scene where wisdom did not reign.
They had ceased to see the glory of the vision
that had led them forth rejoicing ; it had been
dimmed by the mist of worldliness. But now
they had left the world, and the star again
appeared. It had been waiting for them all
along in the pure heavens, and when their
eyes had lost the impurity of earth they
beheld its calm light once more.

So is it ofttimes with thee, my soul. Thou criest out that the glory of other days has departed, and that the star of Bethlehem has set, when all the time it is thou that hast departed from the glory. The star has never left the sky, but thou hast lost sight of the sky. Thy vision has become bounded by the forms and pageants of what men call the great world, and thou canst not recall the glow of other days. But if thou shalt depart from the contact of worldliness thy star shall reappear. If thou shalt leave the form and the pageants thou shalt see the calm light that made thy earth a heaven. The glory of thy East shall be given back to thee—the glory of the days when thou wert young, and when the heart of thy youth bounded as the roe. Thy star waits for thee, waits to lead thee to the manger of the child-Christ; and when thou shalt reach the humility of Bethlehem thou shalt be thyself a child again—a child in heart, a man in wisdom.

IX.

WALKING WITH GOD.

" And all the days of Enoch were three hundred sixty and five years: and Enoch walked with God: and he was not ; for God took him."—GEN. v. 23, 24.

GREAT men, it hath been said, have short biographies. So is it with Enoch. He is the greatest figure of that old world, head and shoulders above all the antediluvians, yet his was the shortest life of all. The number of his outward years does not attain to the number of the years of his fathers ; there is less to tell of him than of them. Why is there less to tell? It is because he is greater than they. His life was more inward, and therefore it was more hidden. The part that lived most intensely was just the part which men do not see—the spirit, the heart, the soul. His life was hid with God, because in its essence it was the life of God—love. It was too inward a life to make an impression on the world ; its walk was divine, and therefore it was deemed a lowly walk, a thing to be forgotten. Yet nothing else has been remembered in all that world. Its wars and rumours of wars, its marryings and givings in marriage, its buyings and sellings and banquetings have been numbered with the dead; but Enoch, by his walk with God, is alive for evermore.

My soul, thy walk with God is thy evidence of immortality. What is it that separates thee from the beast of the field? It is the path of duty. There thou walkest with God aloft and alone. Thou hast already a portion unshared by the life of the lower creation. Thou hast transcended the seen and temporal; thou hast entered the unseen and eternal, thou hast passed from death unto life. No human theory can rob thee of thy hope. It is not a hope, it is not a faith, it is not even a proof; it is a sight, a fact, an experience, a life begun. Thy hope of glory is Christ already in thee. Thou art immortal before death. Thou hast reached even now the promised land, and canst look smiling from the other bank of Jordan. When death shall come to seek thee, he shall see thee already escaped from the

B

fowler's snare, and shall write this verdict of
his own discomfiture, " He was not found; for
God took him."

X.

GOD'S DWELLING-PLACE.

" In Him dwelleth all the fulness of the Godhead bodily."
—COL. ii. 9.

" WHERE does God live?" asks the little
child; " Oh that I knew where I might find
Him!" cries the earnest man. We are all
seeking Thy dwelling-place, thou King of
kings. We have not yet found a palace large
enough to contain Thee. Some have sought
Thee in the water, some in the air, some in
the fire, because the water and the air and the
fire are to us boundless things. Yet it is not
in the boundless that Thou desirest to be
found; it is in the limited, the broken, the
contrite. The heaven of heavens cannot contain Thee, but the broken and the contrite
heart can; it is there Thou delightest most to

dwell. Thy brightest glory is not in the stars, but in the struggles of a conquering soul. Thy temple is the heart of Him,whom men have called the Man of sorrows. Thy fulness dwells in His emptiness, Thy wealth in His poverty, Thy strength in His weakness, Thy joy in His sorrow, Thy crown in His cross. Within that temple meet harmoniously the things which to the world are discords— perfection and suffering, peace and warfare, love and storm; the lion and the lamb lie down together. There would I seek Thee, O my God. Within these sacred precincts, where all things are gathered into one, where middle walls of partition are broken down, where jarring chords are blended in one symphony of praise, there would I seek and find Thee. Under the shadow of that cross, where death meets life and earth is touched by heaven, my finite soul would lose its finitude and be one with Thee. My night would vanish in Thy day, my sorrow would melt in Thy joy, my meanness would merge in Thy majesty, my sin would be lost in Thy holiness. The veil which hides me from Thee is the shadow of

my own will; when the veil of the temple shall be rent in twain I shall see the place where Thy glory dwelleth.

XL

THE WILDERNESS AFTER JORDAN.

" Then was Jesus led up of the Spirit into the wilderness."
—MATT. iv. 1.

THEN was Jesus led up. Surely it was a strange time for such a catastrophe. Was it not just after the glorious vision on the banks of Jordan, when the heavens had been opened to His sight, and the dove-like Spirit had descended on His soul, and the Father's voice had sounded in His ear, " This is my beloved Son, in whom I am well pleased." After such a vision, after such a voice, one would have thought that there was no room in His life for a wilderness any more ; yet it was then, and at no other time, that the wilderness appeared. I too have betimes been forced to repeat this experience of my Lord. I have

sat down at the table of communion, and it
has seemed to me as if heaven were for ever
opened. All clouds have vanished from my
path, and the silence has been broken by the
benediction of a Father's voice, and the dove-
like Spirit has whispered in my ear the promise of a peace that passeth knowledge. But
then anon the shadows have gathered anew.
The table of communion has been withdrawn,
and the Divine voice has seemed to be silent,
and that which was once the garden of the
Lord has been transformed into the solitudes
of the wilderness. I have asked myself in
surprise wherefore my soul has been thus disquieted. Why has the glory of my morning
faded? Why has the glad promise of peace
been broken? I went out, like the Psalmist,
with a multitude that kept holyday, and I
have returned alone. Why art Thou so far
from helping me, O my God?

My soul, thou art disquieted without a cause.
Thy God is not far from helping thee; thy
God has never left thee for a moment; He
has passed with thee from the Jordan into the
wilderness. It is the *Spirit* that leads thee

Peace from the storm

Peace in the storm

up into the wilderness. He would not have
fulfilled His promise of peace had He left thee
on the banks of Jordan. The vision of the
opened heavens was only peace *from* the
storm, but the promise He made to thee was
a promise of peace *in* the storm. That promise He can only keep in the wilderness.
What proof wouldst thou have of His love?
Wouldst thou have purple and fine linen, and
sumptuous faring every day? That would
not be a peace which passeth knowledge ; it
would be a peace explainable by earthly
causes. But if the clouds should gather, if
the stars should go out, if the night winds
should blow and beat upon the house of thy
life, and if through all that life should be
strong and steadfast, then verily thou hast a
peace not given by the world—a peace independent of the earth, defiant of the wilderness.
If the dove that lighteth from the opened
heavens can abide when the heavens have
been closed, thy bright experience at Jordan
shall be proved to be no dream.

XII.

TEMPTATION.

" And the devil, taking Him up into an high mountain, showed unto Him all the kingdoms of the world in a moment of time."—LUKE iv. 5.

THE tempter had tried the Son of Man through the power of depression ; he now tries Him by the power of exaltation. He had sought to vanquish Him by the scourge of poverty ; he now seeks to overcome Him by the vision of plenty. He had brought Him down into the valley and had tempted Him by the dangers of humiliation ; he now carries Him up to the mountain and tempts Him by the dangers of elevation. And so the tempter has unwittingly been teaching my heart a lesson. I thought in the days of old that temptation belonged to certain circumstances ; I blamed my cross for my sins. I said within myself that if I could only get a changed cross I would immediately get a changed life, that if I could be freed from the burden and heat of the day I would be freed from the sin that so easily besets me. I did not know that I did not get my sin *from* my circumstances, but that I gave my sin *to* my circumstances. Why was the Son of Man superior to all circumstances ? It was only because He was superior to all sin.· Had there been sin in His heart the valley would have had the same chance as the mountain. The sinful heart will incarnate itself in everything, and will find in everything a temptation. It will be tempted by poverty and it will be tempted by wealth ; it will be in danger from the stones of the desert, and it will be in danger from the kingdoms of the world and their glory. But the sinless heart will be free from temptation everywhere. It will neither be seduced by the exigencies of the valley of humiliation nor by the allurements of the mountain of elevation ; it will not turn the stones into bread to avoid the famine, it will not bow the knee to Baal to purchase a crown.

O Thou Divine Spirit, that hast proved Thy strength alike over the valley and over the mountain, let me find my strength in Thee.

I need Thee, that I may be strong everywhere. I long to be independent of all circumstances, alike of the cloud and of the sunshine. I want a power to keep me from being depressed in the vale and to prevent me from being giddy on the height; to save me from sinking in despondency and to rescue me from soaring in pride. I want both a pillar of fire and a pillar of cloud; a refuge from the night of adversity and a shield from the day of prosperity. 1 can find them in Thee. Thou hast proved Thy power both over the night and over the day; Thou hast vanquished the tempter in the valley and Thou hast conquered the tempter on the hill. Come into my heart, and Thy power shall be my power. The earth shall be mine and the fulness thereof. I shall be victorious over all circumstances, at home in all scenes, restful in all fortunes. I shall have power to tread upon scorpions, and they shall do me no hurt; the world shall be mine when Thy Spirit is in me.

———

XIII.

CANA OF GALILEE.

" This beginning of miracles did Jesus in Cana of Galilee, and manifested forth His glory, and His disciples believed on Him."—JOHN ii. 11.

STRANGE place for the first manifestation of the Son of Man ! He had conquered the tempter in the solitudes of the wilderness, the place where one should have least expected that the tempter would be found, and now He comes to seek him in that world which is supposed to be his natural sphere. Why did He not remain in that wilderness which He had made beautiful ? Why did He not rest in the solitudes of that scene which He had made a scene of unruffled contemplation ? It was because the design of conquering temptation is to make us fit for the world. We do not conquer in order that we may rest, we conquer in order that we may work. We are brought up into the solitudes, not that we may avoid the world, but that we may prepare for the world. We are made to feel our loneliness only that we may be trained for not being alone. We get our glory that we may manifest our glory. Our glory is the choice of Christ over the kingdoms of the world, and we can only make it in the secret places of the soul; but when we have made it, the kingdoms of the world become our sphere. The Son of Man refused to turn the stones into bread, but that refusal gave Him a right to turn the water into wine. He was fit for the world because He had shown Himself to be unworldly.

My soul, often hast thou asked thyself if it is right for thee to frequent the common haunts of men; if it would not be better for thee to get away from the scenes and pursuits of the madding crowd. Nay, but, my soul, who art thou that askest? Everything depends on the answer to that question. What has been thy past experience? Has it been frivolous or has it been earnest? Has thy life been hitherto knit to the things that are perishable? Then thou art not fit to live amongst these things: they are too strong for thee, they will drag thee down to their own level. But hast thou passed through the solitudes of the wilderness? Hast thou in the strength of the Son of Man made choice already of the strait gate and the narrow way? Hast thou in the silence of the heart preferred the path of duty to the way of pleasure, and the rule of principle to the reign of passion? Then thou hast received a key to open all the doors of life; thou hast liberty to do all things if Christ has strengthened thee. The world has become thine by reason of thine unworldliness. Thou hast received more freedom of spiritual diet than is allowed to the worldly mind. Thou canst bear more things without hurt than the worldling can. Thou canst frequent more scenes without detriment than the worldling dare. Cana of Galilee shall be open to thy steps. All the relationships of life shall be endeared to thee. All the pleasures of life shall be sweetened to thee. All the pursuits of life shall be hallowed to thee. All the burdens of life shall be ennobled to thee. The Light that is in thee is a light to lighten the Gentiles as well as the glory of God's people Israel; for he that has prevailed with God has power also over man.

XIV.

HEAVEN WITHOUT A TEMPLE.

*"And I saw no temple therein: for the Lord God
Almighty and the Lamb are the temple of it."*—Rev.
xxi. 22.

No temple therein ; are these words a promise
or a threat ?   Heaven without a temple seems
a strange boon.   Heaven without pain, heaven
without death, heaven without sorrow or sigh-
ing,—all this I can understand ; but heaven
without a temple—is it not nature without a
sun ?   Nay, verily, rather is it nature without
a cloud.   What the seer means to describe is
not a heaven where there shall be no religion,
but a heaven where there shall be nothing *but*
religion, where religion shall be all in all.   The
Jewish temple circumscribed the range of
man's worship.   It said, Thou shalt worship
here but not there, to-day but not to-morrow,
in the sacred but not in the secular, in the
burnt-offering but not in the hourly offering

of the will.   But the vision of heaven without
a temple spoke volumes.   It said, All places
are holy, all days are holy, all duties are holy.
Every spot whereon thou treadest is henceforth
sacred.   Say not, I must give one portion of
my time to God; thy God claims all thy time
—thy heart and soul and strength and mind.
Say not, I must cease betimes from work that
I may worship; thy work must itself be a
worship, a rest in God.   Hast thou pondered
the meaning of these words, "The Lord thy
God is a jealous God?"   God's love for thee
is too divine to be satisfied with the fragments
of thy heart; He must have all or nothing.
He will not accept from thee the mere pauses
in thy pursuit of pleasure, the mere breathing-
spaces in thy race of ambition; He will have
thee to find Him everywhere.   He will not let
thee call one house His edifice if thereby all
other houses be profaned.   His temple is an
universal temple.   Its height is the summit of
heaven, its depth is the base of sacrifice, its
length is the measure of eternity, its breadth
is the vastness of every finite need, its glory
is the glory of the Lamb.

O Thou, whose love is not confined to temples made with hands, enlarge my heart to worship Thee. Help me to see Thee where men see only the world, to hear Thee where men hear only the voices of the crowd. Enlarge the range of my reverence. Teach me to realise the awful solemnity of the things which I call common. Impress me with the truth that the meanest household duty is a service of Thee, that the smallest act of kindness is a praise of Thee, that the tiniest cup of water, though it were given only in a disciple's name, is a worship and a love of Thee. Help me to feel the sense of Thy presence everywhere, that even in the prosaic haunts of men and in the commonplace battles of life I may be able to lift up mine eyes and say, "This is none other than the house of God, this is the gate of heaven."

XV.

NO MORE SEA.

" There was no more sea."—Rev. xxi. 1.

HUMAN life below has more sea than land. It is not a connected continent—a brotherhood of souls; it is a multitude of little islands divided by stormy waves. There is a great gulf fixed between my life and the life of my brother—the gulf of self-interest; I cannot pass over to him, and he cannot pass over to me. And the secret of our separation is the secret also of our unrest. We live in perpetual storms because we live in perpetual selfishness; the wave of our thoughts rolls back upon ourselves. But in that higher life which the seer of Patmos saw the gulfs were all dried up, and the separation of land from land appeared no more. Human nature became to his gaze a continent. Men lost their isolation and ran together into unity. They saw eye to eye, they felt heart to heart, they wrought hand to hand, and the glory of the Lord was revealed

because all flesh could see it together. Each
man took up the trouble of his brother-man,
and in taking the trouble of his brother each
man lost his own. There came a great stillness
over the individual heart. Its stillness came
because its burden fell, and its burden fell
because the burdens of humanity rose; there
was perfect self-forgetfulness, therefore there
was no more sea.

O thou Son of Man, who, by lifting the
burdens of our humanity, hast made Thine own
yoke easy and Thine own burden light, lift
this life of mine into sympathy, into union
with Thee. I am weary of myself, weary of
the din and the battle, weary of the burden
and the heat. I am seeking everywhere for a
hiding-place from the storm, everywhere for
a covert from the tempest. But the storm is
not without me, but within; the tempest is
not in my circumstances but in me. Son of
Man, save me from myself, that I may enter
into Thy peace, Thine unspeakable joy. Inspire me with Thine own burden of love, that
the care of self may fall from me, and that with
Thy divine freedom I may be free. Help me

to take up Thy cross, that I myself may be
lifted up. Give me Thy spirit of sacrifice, that
I may be elevated above my own fears.   Unite
me to the great continent, the brotherhood of
human souls, that the storms of my island life
may be lulled to rest ; then shall I be able in
my heart to say, "There is no more sea."

XVI.

WHERE TO MEET WITH GOD.

" *And there I will meet with the children of Israel, and
the tabernacle shall be sanctified by My glory.*"—
Exod. xxix. 43.

" *THERE* I will meet with the children of
Israel."   Where ?   At the door of the tabernacle.   Not *in* the tabernacle, but at the
door.   The service of the sanctuary was to
them to be sanctified and glorified, because
the spirit of worship was to meet them at the
entrance.   They were not to be forced to enter
with a worldly spirit on the chance of finding
light in the progress of the day.   They were

to find light on the threshold that was to
keep them *all* the day—light for the morning
sacrifice, light for the evening incense, light for
the intermediate hours. So has it been with
me. I set out through the problems of life
on a search for God, and I did not find God;
I found only problems that made me doubt of
God. Then I said in words of old, "Verily
Thou art a God that hidest Thyself;" "Why
art Thou so far from helping me?" And
while I yet spake, a voice made answer:
"Why didst thou not meet me at the door?
Thou hast been in search of me through the
labyrinths of the world; why didst thou not
come first to me to lead *thee* through the
labyrinths? Thou hast been seeking to see
me by the light of the world; why didst thou
not rather seek to see the world by my light?
I would have made all things clear to thee
if thou hadst met me at the door. Thou
wouldst not have been surprised by the
mystery of sorrow. I would have shown thee
before starting that life is not a pleasure-
ground, but a school. I would have sanctified
to thee in advance the strait gate and the

narrow way. I would have gone before thee with a pillar of fire to light each cloud by my presence, so that in the valley of every shadow thou wouldst have said, ' Surely the Lord was in this place.' "

My God, it is not too late to begin anew. Let me start again on the path of existence, no longer in search of Thee, but *with* Thee. Let me meet Thee at the door of life, that Thou mayst be my interpreter through all the way. When crosses lie before me and I call them accidents, interpret Thou to me ; show me that the cross is the road to the crown. When weakness overtakes me and I call it failure, interpret Thou to me ; show me that Thy strength is made perfect in weakness. When darkness hovers round me, and I call it the hiding of Thy countenance, interpret thou to me ; show me that with Thee the night is even as the noon. Teach me that all things are good and perfect gifts from Thee—even the terror by night and the arrow that flieth by day. Teach me that Thy love can have no variableness nor the least shadow of turning. Let me believe in Thy love *before* all events, that I may interpret all events *by* thy love. The sacrifices of life's tabernacle shall be sanctified when I have met Thee at the door.

XVII.

THE FIRE OF GOD.

"*And the glory of the Lord appeared unto all the people. And there came a fire out from before the Lord, and consumed upon the altar the burnt offering.*"—LEV. ix. 23, 24.

THERE are two fires to which the soul is subject—the fire of sin, and the fire of God. There is a fire which men call the fire of hell, and there is a fire which they ought to call the fire of heaven ; the one consumes the soul, the other consumes everything that impedes the soul. The fire of sin comes because God is absent, but the fire of God only comes when He Himself is near. So was it with this congregation at the door of the tabernacle. They beheld a consuming fire, but they beheld it not because God was far away, but because

He was verily at the door. It was only when
the glory of God had appeared that the consuming fire appeared. There was no sacrifice
to them, no sense of pain to them, no life-
surrender to them, until their eyes had rested
on the vision of the Divine glory. But when
the vision of God's glory came the consuming fire came too; the sacrifice and the pain
followed the sight of God. "There came a fire
out from before the Lord."

My soul, ponder deeply the meaning of
these words, for they have a deep message for
thee. Often hast thou been called to pass
through the fire, and it has seemed to thee a
hard thing. It has seemed to thee as if thy
God had overlooked thy cause, nay, even as if
thou wert under His special judgment. Didst
thou forget that there is a fire which burns
only the alloy, and burns it for the sake of the
gold? Didst thou forget that there is a suffering which means not enmity but fellowship
with thy God? Didst thou forget that he who
follows closest after the life Divine is ever he
who is nearest to the cross. There are sacrifices which can only begin with the Christ-life,

offerings which can only be made in the presence of the Infinite Glory. The fire of heaven
was God's first gift to thee; it consumed the
dross and disencumbered the precious ore. It
shall ever be to thee a memory of joy, for,
walking in the midst of the furnace, was One
like unto the Son of Man.

XVIII.

CHRISTIAN ASPIRATION.

" I shall be satisfied, when I awake, with Thy likeness."—
Ps. xvii. 15.

AND shall nothing less than *this* content thee,
O Psalmist? To awake in the likeness of God,
—it is a bold aspiration for a frail and sinful
mortal. I should rather have expected thee
to have crouched down in absolute humiliation
before the blaze of the Infinite Glory. I
should have expected thee to have asked only
the crumbs that should fall from the Master's
table, to have been content with the smallest
token of the Master's recognition. Why didst

thou not ask merely to be made one of the hired servants in the house of thy God, to be assigned the position of a pardoned and reinstated slave? Instead of that, thy demand is insatiable, inexhaustible. There is no limit to its soaring, there is no bound to its desire. It will not be content with the remission of a penalty, it will not be appeased with the promise of pardon, it will not even be perfectly gratified with the message of reconciliation, it must have union with God Himself. It aspires to be one with the life and will of the Highest; it gazes into the Infinite Brightness and cries, "I shall be satisfied, when I awake, with Thy likeness."

My soul, the Psalmist is in this a type of thee at thy best. Whenever thou art near to God thy demands are insatiable. It is when thou art far from God that thine expectations are small; the narrow heart has a short outlook. It is when thy heart is enlarged that thy wants are enlarged; thy wants are the measure of thee, thy want of God is most of all the measure of thee. When God has come near to thee thou wilt accept no compromise.

Thou wilt not be satisfied with His outward gifts, thou wilt not be contented with His promise of pardon ; thou shalt have Himself alone It will not appease thee to be told that there is no more *fear* ; thou shalt insist to enter into the *joy* of thy Lord. Thou shalt ask to see as He sees, to will as He wills, to know as He knows. Thou shalt claim the privilege of a kindred spirit, whereby thou mayest commune with Him as a man talketh with his friend.; and when the world wonders that thou art not at rest in the possession of its own gifts, thou shalt point thy finger upward and say, " I shall be satisfied, when I awake, with *His* likeness."

XIX.

CHRIST'S SYMPATHY.

"*I have compassion on the multitude, because they have now been with me three days, and have nothing to eat : and if I send them away fasting to their own houses, they will faint by the way.*"—MARK viii. 2, 3.

THE compassion here displayed by the Son of Man is a pity for the common wants of men.

It is their *common* wants that here impress Him. He is not afraid for this multitude as to its spiritual condition; He knows that the men who compose it are intensely spiritual. But He fears that the very intenseness of their spiritual excitement has made them forget their temporal necessities. They have been enduring physical privation, but they have not felt it because their thoughts have been away from themselves; their thoughts and their eyes have been on *Him.* But He knows that the moment they shall lose sight of Him their physical privation shall exert itself; He knows that the moment He has sent them away from His presence they shall feel that physical want which they now have without feeling it, and His human heart bleeds for the human needs of man.

O Thou Son of Man, in Thy religion alone is there hope for those who toil. Thou alone of all masters hast sympathy with the needs of the common day, with the wants of the passing hour. To all other masters the needs of the common day are ignoble, the wants of the passing hour are sin. The religions of men have no sympathy with man *as* man; they call on him to leave the world, they frown upon his struggles for the perishable bread. But Thou hast compassion on the prosaic toilers of life. Thou hast compassion on those who are fasting by the way, and who have no spiritual vision to break their fast. Thou hast compassion on the crowd in which each man is alone—alone with his solitary battle, alone with his poverty and care. Thou hast taken up the cross of them that labour, and hast claimed it for Thine own. Thou hast identified Thine interest with the cry of struggling millions: "Give us this day our daily bread."

XX.

GOD'S WARNING.

"But if ye will not do so, behold, ye have sinned against the Lord: and be sure your sin will find you out."—Num. xxxii. 23.

SHOULD we not have expected a fiercer denunciation, a stronger form of Divine threatening? Should we not have looked for such words as

these, "If ye will not do so, behold, ye have
sinned against the Lord, and the thunderbolt
of the Lord will strike you?" Does it not
seem a lame and impotent conclusion to tell
these men merely that if they broke the
Divine command the result of their sin would
one day overtake them, that the seed of their
own sowing would one day be a seed of bitterness? Is this mild language consistent with
our thought of the majesty of God? Nay,
verily, for we have never thought worthily of
that majesty. We have thought of Him as a
being who shall destroy us if we do not obey
Him. It is not He that shall destroy, it is ourselves; He wants to *save* us from ourselves.
His is not a threatening, it is a warning—a
warning whose fulfilment He would deplore
more than we. Wherefore does He say, "In
the day that thou eatest thereof thou shalt
surely die"? Not because *He* is vindictive,
but because sin is mortal. Thy sin carries her
sting in her own bosom, and the infinite love
that is hid in the bosom of the Father yearns
to find it and to extract it ere it shall find and
destroy thee.

O Love unspeakable and full of glory, whose majesty is not to destroy but to save, save me from myself. My past relentlessly pursues me. Days that I thought dead live over again, deeds that I deemed buried meet me on the way ; be thou my rearward, O my God. Fill up that which my life has left behind, undo that which my life has done amiss. Repair the places I have wasted, bind the hearts I have wounded, dry the eyes I have flooded. Make the evil I have done to work for good, so that I myself would not know it. Overrule the acts I did in malice ; weave them into Thy Divine mosaic, that my very wrath may be made to praise Thee. Take up my yesterdays into Thine own golden light, and transfigure them there, that I may learn with joyful surprise how even against my will I was labouring together with Thee ; so shall my former self find me no more.

XXI.

THE GROUND OF IMMORTALITY.

" Art Thou not from everlasting, O Lord my God, mine
Holy One ? we shall not die."—HAB. i. 12.

PRESUMPTUOUS words these surely from the
creature to the Creator : " Thou art from
everlasting, therefore *I* shall not die." What
right have I to measure my life with *Him ?*
He is from everlasting ; I am of yesterday.
He has the dew of His youth ; my days de-
cline as doth a shadow. He is the same
yesterday, to-day, and for ever ; my life is
changed as a vesture every hour. Would it
not be more becoming for me to say, " Thou
art from everlasting, therefore *I* must die."
Nay, my soul, thou hast not rightly read the
ground of thine own hope. The prophet is
not seeking to have his own life made equal
to God's ; he is seeking to have God's own
life in *him.* Bethink thee what mean such
words as these, " Because 1 live, ye shall live
also ; " " I live, yet not I, but Christ liveth in
me ; " " Christ in you, the hope of glory."

They mean that thy immortality is God's immortality. Thy hope of vanquishing death is thy possession in thyself of the deathless One. It is because the Everlasting is *thy* God that His everlastingness is anything to thee. Were He merely outside of thee it would be indeed presumption in thee to measure thy years with Him. But He is not outside of thee. He has breathed into thy nostrils the breath of His own life, and it is by that breath that even now thou livest. It is by that breath that even now thou art victor over death from moment to moment, from hour to hour, from day to day. It is by that breath that, when flesh and heart faint and fail, thou shalt be victor over death still, shalt find the strength of thy heart and thy portion for ever.

Spirit of Christ, Spirit in whose breath I live and move and have my being, reveal day by day the power of Thy presence within me. Reveal to me that the power of Thy presence is the power of my resurrection, the certitude of my immortality. Ofttimes I stand aghast before the gates of the great mystery; I wonder what things shall be in the state

after death.   Teach me that the state after
death exists already before death, that I need
not taste of death until I have seen the
kingdom of God.   Teach me that my immortality is not to come, that it is here, that
it is now.   Teach me that the life eternal
is not merely the life *beyond* the grave, but
the life on this side the grave.   Reveal to me
that I am *now* in eternity, that I am breath-
ing the very air of those that have passed the
gates.   Let me have more than hope; give
me fruition.   Let me feel that I am already
immortal; that death could no more destroy
my life than it could destroy Thine, because
mine *is* Thine.   When my strength is weakened
in the way, when the shadows of the grave
seem to encompass me, help me to remember
not so much that there is a life above as that
there is a life within.   Help me to remember,
not that Thou art waiting for me across the
valley, but that Thou art waiting with me *in*
the valley; then shall the rod and staff of my
comfort be, "Thou art from everlasting, therefore I shall not die."

XXII.

REVELATION.

" Open Thou mine eyes, that I may behold wondrous things out of Thy law."—Ps. cxix. 18.

WHEREFORE is it, my soul, that in thy cry for revelation thou lookest ever to the rending of an outer veil ? It seems to thee that if there could only be a parting of the clouds, thou wouldst have a vision of things unutterable, that if thou couldst be transplanted *beyond* the clouds, the glory of the Lord would be revealed. And so it is to death thou lookest as the great revealer, to that hour when the silver cord shall be loosed and the golden bowl shall be broken. Nay, my soul, but thou art looking too far for thy revelation. Thou dost not need to wait for the loosing of the silver cord or the breaking of the golden bowl. What thou needest is not a new scene, but a new sense. There are beauties undisclosed lying at thy feet waiting for that sense to come. The prayer for thee is : "Open Thou mine

D

eyes, that I may behold wondrous things." The wondrous things of thy God are already around thee ; they are lying at the door of thy being, they are touching the hem of thy garment. To see them thou dost not need to be transplanted either by life or by death. Thou dost not need to change thy place even by an hair's-breadth ; thou hast want only of an eye. One other spiritual sense would make to thee a new universe, another world without and within. It would clothe the woods in fresh verdure, it would paint the flowers in new beauty, it would gild the sunbeams in unwonted glory. It would throw light upon dark places of creation, it would illuminate unfrequented depths of thought, it would make clear in a moment, in the twinkling of an eye, problems that have wrung the heart with pain. What thinkest thou mean these words, " And Abraham lifted up his eyes, and looked, and behold, *behind* him a ram caught in a thicket "? He had been perplexing his mind as to where he should find a burnt-offering—a substitute for his own pain ; this ram caught in the thicket came to him as a revelation. Yet

whence came the revelation ? Only from the
lifting up of his eyes. The ram had all along
been in that thicket ; he merely needed to see
it. While he had been waiting for his consolation, his consolation had been waiting for
him. The boon which he sought was already
" behind him ; " he had passed it by on the
way. When he opened his eyes what he saw
was his own *past*—the glory of something
which had escaped him on the journey. Even
so, my soul, is it with thee. There are pas-
sages of God's law, written and unwritten,
which thou art passing heedlessly by, which
thou hast perused without interest as slight
and commonplace things. One day thou shalt
know that thou hast been in contact with
angels unawares. One day thou shalt know
that what thou hast passed by on the way
was a treasure of purest gold. Thou too, like
Abraham, shalt look behind thee and find in
these neglected things the remedy for all thy
pain ; when thine eye shall open upon thy
past thou shalt awake to the vision of its
wondrous glory.

XXIII.

THE INWARDNESS OF REVELATION.

" To reveal His Son in me."—GAL. i. 16.

ST. PAUL is here describing the process of his own conversion, the light which he saw from heaven. He says that it pleased God to reveal His Son in him. Why *in* him? Wherefore does he not say, " It pleased God to reveal His Son *to* me "? Was not the light which he saw an outer vision? Did it not arrest him at midday with a glory above the brightness of the sun? Did it not bar the way to his old nature, and bid his life to pause in the midst of his journey? Surely that picture of his Lord was a vision to his eye. Nay, but can any picture be a vision to the eye? Can a thing be revealed *to* me which has not been revealed *in* me? Is the landscape on which I gaze revealed only to my outward vision? Nay, or it would not be revealed at all; there could be no beauty without if there were not a sense of beauty within. Is the music to which I listen revealed only to my outward ear ? Nay, or I would be deaf to it for evermore ; there could be no harmony without if there were not a sense of harmony within. So is it with the beauty of Him who is fairer than the children of men. Often have I envied the lot of those who were permitted to gaze upon His outward form, to see the beam on His face, to hear the thrill in His voice. Yet was it not the very chief of these to whom the words were spoken, "Flesh and blood hath not revealed it unto thee." It was not the *eye* which saw the beam, it was not the *ear* which heard the thrill ; it was the soul, the heart, the life, the responsive spirit bearing witness with His Spirit, the kindred sympathy that ran out to meet its counterpart, and found in Him all its salvation because it found in Him all its desire.

My God, reveal Thy Son in me. I ask for more than an audible voice, because I need more. It would not help me to behold Thy handwriting on the clouds of heaven ; it would be but the letters of a book to the child that cannot read. Teach me the meaning of Thy words.   No description of Thy heavens could declare their glory to the born blind ; no description of Thy Christ could manifest His greatness to the loveless soul.   Therefore, O Spirit of love, breathe into this heart the new sensation of loving, the new experience of *being* loved.   Inspire this consciousness with that thought which transcends all the channels of the natural sense.   Unseal the inner eye, unstop the spiritual ear, that the symmetries and the harmonies of all worlds may be revealed.   It is in Thy light alone that we shall see light.   Only they who are rooted and grounded in love shall be able to comprehend that love of Thine, which, although familiar to all saints, passeth finite knowledge.   I shall see the King in His beauty when His beauty shall be revealed in me.

XXIV.

DESERT EXPERIENCES.

"*And the angel of the Lord spake unto Philip, saying, Arise, and go toward the south, unto the way that goeth down from Jerusalem unto Gaza, which is desert.*"—ACTS viii. 26.

" ARISE, and go unto the way which is desert." Startling words these to be addressed by an angel of goodness to an earnest human soul. They would be startling if addressed to any man, but they are specially so when spoken to a man of God. To tell the zealous missionary to go into the desert, to bid the seeker of souls to frequent that spot where souls are least expected to be, it was surely a strange, an unprecedented mandate. Nay, not unprecedented; it has its parallel in your life and mine. How often in the midday of our career has an arresting hand seemed to bar our progress, has an arresting voice seemed to say, " Hitherto shalt thou go, and no further." My strength was weakened in the way at the very moment

new light on the old circumstances

and Thy truth; let *them* lead me." He does not ask for new circumstances, but for a new light on the old circumstances. Thou who art weighted with some heavy burden, pause ere thou askest its removal; thy weight of present care may be thy weight of future glory—may be, nay, must be when light shall dawn. When thou wert a child, study was a weight of care to thee; now that thou art a man, it is a weight of glory; thou comfortest thyself that thou wert able to endure. So shall it be with the tasks of the larger school. One day thou shalt look back and find them to have been all very good. From the light of thy seventh morning thou shalt look back, from the summit of the finished creation thou shalt behold thy six days of toil, and there shall be no night there. Thy past shall be glorious when it *is* past. Thou shalt retrace the steps of thy way, and find them to have been the steps to thy Sabbath of rest. Thou shalt weigh in the balance the former days, and they shall weigh even heavier than of yore; but that which was once a weight of care shall be then a weight of glory.

XXVIII.

THE POWER OF CHRIST'S SACRIFICE.

" Therefore doth my Father love me, because I lay down my
life. . . . No man taketh it from me. . . . I have
power to lay it down."—JOHN x. 17, 18.

"THEREFORE doth my Father love me." What
is this secret of the Father's love ? Why is it
that the heart of the Father rejoices in the
Son ? Is it because of the pain of the Son's
sacrifice ? Is it because His Father beheld in
Him a victim on the altar of death ? Nay, it
is because on the altar of death He beholds
in Him an offering that is no victim. The
Father's heart rejoices not that the Son is compelled to die, but that the Son can die without
compulsion, that He has power to lay down
His life. All other sacrifices had been types
of impotence, but this was a type of power.
Never had the strength of will been manifested
so gloriously. There had been great conquerors and mighty warriors, who had paved
their own way through the hearts of others;

E

here was a life that could pave a way for
others through its own heart. O strength
perfected in weakness, O self-surrendering
power of love, we, like the Father, yield our
hearts to Thee.   If it had been mere resignation to death we could have admired Thee; if
it had been the mere distaste for life we could
have pitied Thee; but since it is the choice of
love we love Thee.   We magnify the power
that could relinquish power, the might that
could abandon might, the will that could
resign will.   Thou art most crowned to us in
the valley of Thy humiliation.   Thou art most
glorious to us in the shades of Thy Gethsemane.   We feel that Thou art no victim,
that Thy love has chosen the burden, that
Thou wouldst not have it otherwise for twelve
legions of angels.   Therefore Thy cross is to
us not a weakness but a power; we are not
ashamed of it, we glory in it, we long to be
like it.   We pant to be made conformable
unto Thy death, to have our wills set free
from their own burning.   We gaze on Thee
till we shall catch Thine impress, till we shall
be transformed into Thine image from glory to

glory, till we shall say, not with resignation but with acquiescence, "Thy will be done." We shall get back our joy the moment we have ceased to seek it; when we shall have power to lay down our life we shall have power to take it again.

XXIX.

THE SECRET OF PEACE.

" He maketh me to lie down in green pastures ; He leadeth me beside the still waters ; He restoreth my soul."— Ps. xxiii. 2, 3.

ONE is apt to say, it was an easy thing for a man with such an experience to confess the Lord to be his Shepherd; who would not rejoice in a God who should make him to lie down in green pastures? Yet, in truth, he who says thus has not sounded the depths of his own being. No man can lie down anywhere until he has received a restored soul. It is as difficult for the unrestored soul to lie down in green pastures as to lie down in barren wastes.

Thinkest thou that an unrestful heart **will**
have more rest in prosperity than in adversity?
Nay, verily, it will carry itself into everything.
Prosperity lies not in the greenness of the
pastures, adversity lies not in the barrenness
of the wastes; they both lie within.   The
joyous heart will make all things joyful; its
pastures will all be green, and its waters will
all be quiet.   The restless heart will make all
things unrestful; the very calmness of its
outward world will become its source of pain.
We cannot fly from ourselves by changing our
circumstances; we can only change our circumstances by flying from ourselves.   The sweetness and the bitterness of life are alike within
us, and we shall get from the world just what
we bring to it.   Therefore, my soul, if thou
wouldst have green pastures, if thou wouldst
have quiet waters, if thou wouldst have any
spot at all wherein thou canst lie down and
rest, then must thou thyself be first restored.
Thou must be set at rest from thine own selfishness ere any place can be to thee a scene of
repose.   Thou must thyself be filled ere the
fulness of the earth can be thine, yea, ere the

[margin notes: unrestful heart; Sweetness and bitterness of life; Prosperity and Barrenness; Green pastures and quiet waters]

emptiness of the earth can be thine. Thou
hast a claim to the earth's emptiness as well
as to its fulness. If thou art at rest all
things are thine—the world, life, death, angels,
principalities, powers; thou canst claim them
as thy possessions, thou canst command them
as thy servants. The winds are thy messengers,
the fires are thy ministers, the clouds are thy
chariots; thou canst extract joy out of sorrow.
Thou shalt sleep in the ship of life when the
storm is raging around thee. Thou shalt
spread thy table in peace in the presence of
thine enemies, and shalt fail to perceive their
enmity. Thy calm shall reflect itself. Thou
shalt see it mirrored in the face of creation,
and the face of creation shall to thee be
beautiful; it shall answer back thy smile.
All the days of thy life goodness and mercy
shall follow thee when thou thyself hast been
restored.

XXX.

THE OMNIPRESENT GOD.

" Thou hast beset me behind and before, and laid Thine hand upon me."—Ps. cxxxix. 5.

In three directions hast Thou beset me, O God. Thou art behind me, Thou art before me, Thou art in contact with me. Thou art behind me in my past, Thou art before me in my future, Thou art in contact with me in the pressure of my present hour. In all these relations I need Thee every day. I am bound to three worlds, and any one of them would crush me were I not beset by Thee. I am bound to the past, and its. chain oppresses me; I am bound to the future, and its shadows appal me; I am bound to the present, and its conflict perturbs me. I want rest for my threefold self—rest in Thee. Beset my dark past with Thy presence; take up its clouds and turn them into sunshine. Beset my shadowy future with Thy glory; reveal the rainbow of Thy promise to the eye of faith.

Beset my arduous present with the sense of
Thy nearness; let me feel laid on me the
pressure of Thy hand. I care not though the
pressure be heavy if only it be Thine; the
yoke that comes from Thee is ever easy, the
burden that Thou sendest is ever light. I
know that wheresoever Thy presence is felt
there is experienced a sense of weight, the
laying on of an invisible hand, but I know,
too, that the weight is of gold. I would not be
without it if I could; it is that which men
call responsibility, and it tells me that I am a
man. I may never again have the carelessness
of the child, for it is a solemn thing to know
that I am with Thee. But there is something better than the carelessness of the child;
it is the carefulness of a spirit weighted with
a sense of God. Therefore, O Lord, impress
me with the magnitude, with the solemnity,
with the awfulness of being a man. Teach
me that I am not my own, that I live not to
myself, that I die not to myself. Lay on me
the weight of my moral obligation. Lay on
me the weight of feeling and knowing that I
am a responsible human soul. Let me hear

the voice of conscience, "You ought, therefore you can." Let me hear the voice of my
brother crying unto me from the ground of
earthly abasement for succour, for solace, for
sustenance. Give me the burden that Thou
hast made golden—the burden of a life that is
straitened till its baptism be accomplished,
oppressed until its work be done. Fill me
with a sense of universal care, that I may
be rendered individually strong ; Thy power
shall be great in me when Thou hast laid on
me Thine hand.

XXXI.

THE SUPERNATURAL IN THE NATURAL.

" And He must needs go through Samaria."—JOHN iv. 4.

HUMANLY speaking, it was all a chapter of
commonplaces. There was nothing in the
meeting at Sychar's well that could not be
explained by natural law. There was no
miracle in the Master going through Samaria ;

He must *needs* go through Samaria, it lay geographically on his way to Galilee. There was no miracle in the Master resting at the well; He must *needs* rest at the well, He was weary and He wanted rest. There was no miracle in the Master finding the woman whom He made His disciple; He must *needs* find her, she was in search of water, and she came to draw. The whole scene was pieced together by the order of natural laws, by the union of natural forces, and each separate event before it happened was just what might have been foreseen. Albeit the mosaic was divine; there was more in the whole than in all the separate parts. Each natural incident was the minister to an end beyond itself—the agent toward a consummation it could not see. The three natural needs made a supernatural result; they brought Divine life into a nation. My soul, do not refuse to see God in the events of thy life because thou canst trace human links between them. Was Peter's vision of the meat from heaven less real because the dream came from his hunger? Nay, for the hunger

and the dream were alike God's messengers to him. Thy treasure is hid in earthen vessels. God speaks to thee in trifles—in the passage through Samaria, in the thirst for earthly water, in the coming to a well. Say not that the little things of thy life are common ; God will cleanse them in the mosaic, they will all be precious in their harmony with the completed whole. Thou shalt see the old deeds pass before thee ; they shall gather themselves together to judgment, and many that are first shall be last, and many that are last shall be first. Valleys shall become mountains in the light of the perfect day. Hours that seemed to be of no account, moments that appeared to be of little value, actions that in their passing were called but ripples in the stream, will be found to have been the tidal wave that led thy life to fortune. Neglect not thy wells of Sychar, O my soul, for where thou seemest to be drawing only earthly water thou mayst be partaking all the time of those living springs whereof they that taste shall never thirst again.

Neglect not thy wells of sychar, O my soul

XXXII.

THE GLORY OF MORNING.

*" And in the morning, then ye shall see the glory of the
Lord."*—EXOD. xvi. 7.

IT is in the morning of life, O Lord, that I
see Thy *glory.* In the midday I see Thy
helpfulness; Thou art then to me the shadow
of a great rock in a weary land, a refuge
from the burden and the heat. In the evening
I see Thy *faithfulness;* I behold the retrospect of all that thou hast done, and lo, it
is all very good. But the morning is the
season of my implicit trust, perfectly implicit
because not yet founded on experience. I
trust Thee at midday because I feel Thy help ;
I trust thee at even because I trace Thy plan,
but I trust Thee at morning without any
reason save the morning's glow in my heart.
I trust Thee as the lark trusts the morning air
into which it soars and through which it sings.
I trust Thee by an instinct of my being. I
trust Thee without experience, before trial,

irrespective of argument, in defiance of difficulty; there is no vision but the brightness
of Thy face.

My God, give me back my youth; I can
regain it in Thee. Let the shadows of my life
be rekindled into morning's glow, let my heart
be lit with Thine eternal youth. Thou hast
promised us eternal life, and what is that? Not
merely life for ever, but life for ever young.
Thine eternal life can make me a child again,
a child without childishness. O Thou, on whose
bloom time breathes not, who art the same
yesterday, and to-day, and for ever, bathe me
in those fountains of the morning whence
Thou hast the dew of Thy youth. Bathe me
in the ocean of that love in which there is no
variableness nor the least shadow of turning,
that the pulses of this heart may be renewed.
Then shall I have the bright and morning
star, and the dayspring from on high shall rise
within me. Then shall creation break forth
into gladness, as in the day when the morning
stars sang together, and all the sons of God
shouted for joy; I shall see the glory of life
when Thy morning is in my soul.

XXXIII.

THE GLORY OF CHRIST.

" *Father, I will that they also whom Thou hast given me be with me where I am ; that they may behold my glory, which Thou hast given me.*"—JOHN xvii. 24.

" WHERE I *am*." Strange place that in which to behold His glory ! We could have understood Him if He had said, "I will that these whom Thou hast given me be with me where I *was*—in the glory which I had with Thee before the foundation of the world." We could have understood Him if He had said, "I will that these whom Thou hast given me be with me where I *shall* be, when Thou shalt glorify me again with Thine own self." But when He says, "be with me where I *am*, that they may behold my glory," we are startled. What glory had He now and here ? Had He not just come to that hour which men called the hour of His humiliation ? was He not on the very borders of the valley of the shadow of death ? Surely it was the last spot where He

should have wished His disciples to behold
His glory. We should have expected Him to
have pointed them on to a time when this
shame would be compensated by the glory to
come; instead of that He says that the glory
has already come, and that He only wishes
they were near enough to see it. He says,
"Father, I wish that these whom Thou hast
given me, these who think this the hour of my
humiliation, could see it as it really is—the
hour of my triumph; I wish they could get so
close to my heart as to behold this hour in the
light that I behold it—the light of a glorious
crown laid on the head of my humanity; then
would their sorrow be turned into joy."

My soul, marvel not at this exaltation in
humiliation; Christ's human glory was His
power to bear. When He said, "Father, the
hour is come; glorify Thy Son, that Thy Son
may glorify Thee," He asked not salvation
from His hour, but strength *in* His hour. He
asked that He might be able to take the cup
with a hand that did not tremble, to say with
a voice that did not falter, "Not as I will, but
as Thou wilt." Canst thou be with Him where

He then was and behold His glory ? Canst thou see the conquest in His stooping, the kinghood in His serving, the greatness in His humility, the crown in His cross ? Canst thou bow down before the majesty of that rod and staff which comforted Him in the valley of the shadow ? Canst thou adore the omnipotence of that strength which could bear the burden of a world without protest, could bear the sins of a world without losing His love for an hour ? Then thou hast reached the privilege which thy Lord desired for thee, for thou hast seen in kindred sympathy with Him that His day of death was His day of glory.

XXXIV.

THE SPIRITUAL YEAR.

" Bringeth forth his fruit in his season."—Ps. i. 3.

THERE are four seasons in thy spiritual year —the winter of desolation; the buds of spring, which tell of hope; the warmth of summer, which bespeaks the fulness of the heart; and the ingathering of autumn, which is the time for life's practical fruits. Each season has its fruit, and the fruit is in its turn golden. Do not seek to change the order of God's spiritual year, do not seek to put the fruits of one season into the lap of another. Thou must not expect the buds of spring from the desolation of winter, for desolation is the fruit of winter; thou, like Nicodemus, must begin thy journey in the sense of night—night without a star. Thou must not expect the warmth of summer from the buds of spring, for the fruit of spring is not fruition but hope; thou, like Peter, must be content for a time to live on aspiration alone. Thou must not expect the practical ingathering of autumn from the warmth of summer, for the fruit of summer is not action but emotion; thou, like John, must be content to lie on the Master's bosom until thy time to work for Him shall come.

O Thou that hast revealed the order of Thine acceptable year, reveal in my experience the stages of that year. Help me to gather the fruits of each season as good and perfect gifts from Thee. When I feel the sense of night, let me accept it as the token that, like

Nicodemus, I am coming to Thee. When I feel the sense of hope, let me accept it as the sign that, like Peter, I am called by Thee. When I feel the sense of warmth, let me accept it as the evidence that, like John, I rest on Thee. When I feel the sense of power and am inspired to gather in the fruits, let me accept it as the pledge that I am bidden, like Paul, to work for Thee. So shall my year be rounded, hallowed, perfected. So shall my life be girt about with Thee. The snows of its winter shall be sanctified, the buds of its spring shall be fostered, the foliage of its summer shall be blest, the first-fruits of its autumn shall be hailed with joy; they shall proclaim that within my soul the year of the Lord has come.   .

XXXV.

THE LIVING WAY.

" By a new and living way."—HEB. x. 20.

IT was a new way because it was a living way. Men had hitherto been seeking in their religion only a dying way. They had thought that Divine worship was something which was good for helping human souls to cross the valley of the shadow ; they had never thought of it as mainly useful in helping human souls to support the shadows of *life*.   But when *He* came He consecrated a new road to God. He told me that I need not wait till the last hour in order to find eternity, that I might find it now.   He told me that God's presence could be reached without dying, that the grandest death of the spirit was the life of love, that the most reasonable service for a man was to present his body a living sacrifice, holy, acceptable unto God.

My Father, shall I offer Thee only my last hours? Teach me Thy living way. Teach me the life of Him who offered up His soul from dawn to dark unceasingly, who poured out on life's altar His childhood, His youth, His manhood, one by one ; who gave Thee in turn His Bethlehem, His Nazareth, His Calvary. Help me to climb with Him the living way. Help me through His Spirit to yield thee my spirit.   Let me not wait to yield it till a dying hour. Give me the power of death in the midst of life, the surrender of the will amid the haunts of men. In the scenes of busy labour, in the paths of anxious toil, in the struggles for daily bread, in the hours of silent trouble, in sorrow and in joy, in sickness and in health, in poverty and in abundance, help me to yield my soul to Thee and say, " Father, into Thy hands I commend my spirit ; " then shall my life on earth be the way to heaven.

XXXVI.

THE PROGRESS OF THE DIVINE LIFE.

" For therein is the righteousness of God revealed from faith to faith."—Rom. i. 17.

From faith to faith ! so runs the course of the Gospel life. Therein is revealed the earthly progress of a divinely-human soul. We see Him rising from peak to peak in the ascent of the mount of God, climbing the spheres of earth from faith to faith. First there is faith in the home life, content to be in subjection, and waiting its time. Next there is faith on the banks of Jordan, dedicating itself to a Father's will. Then comes faith in the wilderness—faith that can prove in temptation the strength of its own vow. By and by there comes a higher test still—faith proved in sorrow, faith under that Gethsemane shadow which hid the very face of God. Lastly, there is faith in death—faith strong in the utmost weakness, crying with a loud voice, " It is finished ! "

O Son of Man, Son of God, who hast been content to rise from the valley of my childhood, let me ascend on steps of Thee. Let me rise through the stages of Thy life from faith to faith. Give me the faith that can wait in obscurity amid the trivial duties of the home life. Give me the faith that can dedicate itself amid the vision of an opened heaven. Give me the faith that can stand on the mount of temptation and see the kingdoms of the world and the glory of them, and say, " Thee only shall I serve." Give me the faith that can enter within the shadows of Gethsemane, and believe in that Father's smile

which it can no longer see. Give me the faith
that can enter that deeper darkness still—the
portals of the grave, and in that hour when
flesh and heart faint and fail can sing with a
loud voice, " O death ! where is thy sting ?
O grave ! where is thy victory ? "

XXXVII.

LOVE CONSTRAINING.

" *The love of Christ constraineth us.*"—2 COR. v. 14.

STRANGE gift this to come from love—constraint, narrowing, imprisonment. I can
understand love enlarging, love liberating,
love bringing out into the boundless expanse
and crowning with the mercies of freedom; but
love *constraining!*—it is a startling, a repel-
ling thought. I have asked myself a thousand
times how the constraints of this world are
to be explained consistently with the love of
God. I have tried a hundred solutions of the
problem how Divine love can co-exist with so
many human limitations, but no solution of

mine ever reached the boldness of this.　I
here told that there is no need of reconciliat
at all, that there is nothing to be reconcil
that between love and constraint there is
ground of controversy.　I am told that c
straint is itself the gift of love,—God's f
gift to my soul.　I am told to see a fri
in that which I held to be an enemy, to cl
as an ally the imagined foe of my hun
happiness.　Love comes to me with a bit
cup in her hand and says, "This cup is
gift to thee: drink thou and be refreshed."

My soul, marvel not that the love of (
should first manifest itself in thy pain.　C
straint is the first gift of all love—even
human fatherhood.　Was not thine eart
childhood developed by sacrifice, by obe
ence to a law whose meaning thou couldst
see?　Did not thine early intelligence exp
through a path of tears, expand through
crushing of thine individual will and
constraint of thine impetuous passions?　1
path of tears was an unconscious rainbow
led thy soul aloft on an arch of triumph.
was only from the summit of the arch t

thou couldst tell how really glorious was thy path of tears. So shall it be with thy larger retrospect. When from the summit of a completed experience thou shalt look back, thou shalt marvel at the glory of the way. The most glorious spots of that way shall just be the spots that, when thou wert passing by, appeared to have no glory. The places which shall be most filled with light shall be thy dark places —the scenes that seemed to thee thy blots on the page of life. Thou shalt see that in these were thy true gifts of fortune. Thou shalt learn that the days called 'adverse were the making of thee, that the seasons of thy spiritual growth were the hours of thy night. And when thou countest up the gifts of Divine love, thou shalt class amongst the brightest of them all those that, in the course of the journey, came to thee as denials of thy prayer; thou shalt look upon the crosses of thy life and say, "The love of Christ constrained me."

XXXVIII.

HUMAN INSTRUMENTALITY.

" *And He took the seven loaves and the fishes, and ga
thanks, and brake them, and gave to His discipl
and the disciples to the multitude.*"—MATT. xv. 36.

AND so there are secondary causes in th
spiritual as well as in the natural worl
Christ was here breaking the bread to th
multitude, but He does not give it to th
multitude directly; He gives it through
medium. He puts it into the hands of th
disciples and tells *them* to give it; the Divir
blessing comes through a secular channel. S
is it ever with the providence of God. H
sends the bread to feed my soul, but He sen
it through earthly ministers, sometimes
earthen vessels. He sends it through th
laws which I call nature's laws, through th
changes which I call life's changes, throug
the troubles which I call the troubles
humanity. He sends it by the most commo
place conveyances, by the most trivial inciden

by the most unlikely contingencies; I am every day, every hour, every moment in the presence of the messengers of God. Do I marvel that the ravens fed Elijah in the wilderness? I am every instant fed by emissaries as untoward as these. All the influences of life, however unpleasing, are in some sense ministering to me; even the lives that come into conflict with mine are unconsciously ministering to mine. The bread from the hands of my God reaches me through the myriad hands of men.

Lord, make me one of Thy secondary causes. I must be so with or without my will, for all things must bend to Thy Divine purpose. But it is not without my will that I desire to serve Thee. I would not be a mere mechanical agent in Thy universe, like the sun by day or the moon and stars by night; I would serve Thee voluntarily, freely, designedly. I would be the conscious distributer of Thy bread to the famished crowd, the conscious minister of Thy strength to the fainting multitude. I would take into my hands the bread which Thou hast broken, and in my turn I would break it anew. I would receive from The Thine own spirit of sacrifice—Thy life broken by love. I would receive from Thee Thine own human burden, the burden of sympathy with the wants and woes of man. I would receive from Thee Thy best, Thy divinest gift —the power and the will to give. Help me to give to others what Thou hast given to me Thou hast given me Thyself. That which Thou hast broken for me is more than the bread; it is Thine own spirit. Give me that spirit of Thine to break for my brother man. Help me to lose myself for him, to forget my self in him, to hide myself in him. Let me be wounded with his wounds, afflicted with his stripes, pained with his sorrows, humiliated with his humiliation. Let me be so identified with him that there shall be one common cross between us, one common load to bear; then shall I break for him the bread Thou hast broken for me.

———————

XXXIX.

THE CHOICE OF MANHOOD.

" *By faith Moses, when he was come to years, refused to be
called the son of Pharaoh's daughter ; esteeming the
reproach of Christ greater riches than the treasures in
Egypt.*"—HEB. xi. 24, 26.

THE reproach of Christ! how could that be
a motive to Moses? Did Moses know anything about Christ? Perhaps not, but he
was bearing His reproach. He was passing
through in anticipation that very choice of
alternatives whose decision constituted the
reproach of his Lord. What *was* the reproach
of Christ? It was His preference of the
internal to the external. He stood on the
mount of temptation, and into each hand
was put a separate cup—into the one a cup
of worldly glory, into the other a cup of
spiritual sacrifice. He chose the latter, and
that was His reproach ; He preferred the service
of His Father to the kingdoms of the world
and the glory of them. Even so did Moses by
the power of the selfsame spirit; he refused

to be called the son of Pharaoh's daughter,
chose rather to go down into the valleys
suffer affliction with the people of God. Un
consciously to himself he was in communication
with the life divinely human, in sympathy
with the spirit of Him who preferred the cross
to the visible crown; he was bearing the reproach of Jesus.

My soul, there is a time when thou too are
called to stand upon the mountain's bro
There is a time when to thee, as to Moses, there
comes a choice of alternatives, when the trea
sures of Egypt lie on the one hand and the
life of sacrifice besets thee on the other. It is
the crisis-hour of all thy life—the hour
which thou hast finished the ascending courage
of youth, and hast reached at its summit the
tableland of manhood. What shall that man
hood be? on thy decision of this choice the
answer must depend. Shall it be a manhood
of visible glitter and empty show, of outward
pomp and selfish ambition, of Judaic priest
and Messianic majesty? or shall it be a man
hood of human care and individual sympathy
of heartfelt responsibility and sacrificial love

of earnest devotion and Christ-like stooping?
This is the latest choice of thy youth, O my
soul. Son of Man, help me to choose with
Thee. Help me to refuse the gold and take
the cross. Help me to go down with Thee
into the valley of humiliation. Help me to
join the band of human sufferers who have
never seen the glory of the mountain's brow.
Let the sense of a common reproach unite my
heart to Thine; so shall my cross be greater
riches than all the treasures of Egypt.

XL.

AN UNSELFISH SEEKING FOR REWARD.

" For he had respect unto the recompense of the reward."—
HEB. xi. 26.

STRANGE conclusion this with which to wind
up the eulogium of a human character. We
have just been told how unselfish has been the
life of Moses, how he has preferred the reproach
of Christ to the treasures in Egypt. And now
we seem to be told that it was but selfishness
after all, that all the time of his sacrifice he

had a motive beyond the sacrifice, that he was seeking the reward of sacrifice. Yes, but what is the reward of sacrifice? It is the power to do good without it. All virtue is at first pain-ful, but if we persevere in the pain it shall at last vanish away, and leave naught but the virtue behind. The reward of sacrifice is the joy of sacrifice; it is the power to say, I once struggled to be unselfish, but it would now be a struggle to be aught beside. It is the joy of getting that as my nature which I once had for my task, of being able to do by instinct what I once performed by rule. The recom-pense of the reward which Moses sought was to be made perfectly unselfish; it was the strength to give more abundantly, to give without pain, without struggle, without re-luctance, without one longing memory of the treasures left behind. And verily that recom-pense was his. Meekness became to him a second nature. The impetuous youth that slew the Egyptian subsided into the man that was content to *be* slain, to die daily for the brotherhood of human souls, to lose even his promised land that Joshua might enter in.

Thou, too, mayst have this recompense. If thou wilt accept the strait gate and the narrow way in its straitness and in its narrowness, it shall ere long become to thee a way of pleasantness and a path of peace. Thou shalt be loosed from the bonds that fetter thine own deeds, loosed not from without but from within. Thy cross shall not be lifted, but it shall be transformed into a crown; thy tasks shall not be remitted, but they shall be transfigured into joys. Thy law shall become thy love, thy duty shall become thy delight, thy service shall become thy freedom. The steep of thy Calvary shall be crowned by the heights of Olivet, and without turning from thy path thou shalt enter into thy glory. When thou hast reached the joy of sacrifice thou hast received the recompense of the reward.

XLI.

THE VOICE IN THE TABERNACLE.

"*And when Moses was gone into the tabernacle of the congregation to speak with Him, then he heard the voice of one speaking unto him from off the mercy-seat.*"—NUM. vii. 89.

WHEN Moses was gone into the tabernacle, *then* he heard the voice. It is not said that the voice then began to speak; rather the contrary is implied. The voice would seem to have been speaking all along, but it was only now that Moses heard it. Why did he hear it now? It was because now for the first time he had put himself in the attitude of hearing. It was when he entered into the tabernacle, it was when he began himself to speak with God, that there woke within him the conviction that God had all the time been speaking with *him*.

My soul, it must be the same with thee. Often art thou crying in the silence of the night that no Divine voice has visited thee.

Nay, but hast thou only listened for it with the
ear of sense ? If so, it is no marvel that thou
hast missed its music. The voice of God
cannot be heard by the ear of sense ; its tones
make no impression on the surrounding air,
they stir not the waves of the earthly atmosphere. Its accents are too still and small to
be caught by the natural ear ; they are speaking incessantly, but they are drowned by
the thunder, the earthquake, and the fire. If
thou wouldst hear them thou must enter the
inner tabernacle, thou must open the inner
ear. Hast thou not read how in the days of
old the miracle was only wrought to faith ?
Why was the miracle only wrought to faith ?
Not because God is narrow, but because truth
is broad. The eye cannot see music, the ear
cannot hear colours ; neither can the natural
receive the spiritual. Faith is the vision of
the soul, the audience-chamber of the soul.
Within its holy temple there are voices in-
numerable—interpreters of all other voices.
Here music waits for thee, here sunbeams
watch for thee, here the mystery of life unveils
herself to be ready for thy coming. When

G

thou shalt enter into the secret of God's
pavilion to speak with Him, there shall break
upon thy heart the wondrous revelation that
all thy life He has been speaking with thee.

***

XLII.

TARRYING UNDER THE CLOUD.

"*And when the cloud tarried long upon the tabernacle
many days, then the children of Israel kept the charge
of the Lord, and journeyed not.*"—NUM. ix. 19.

IT would be well for us if we could repeat this
experience.   *Our* practice is to journey after
the cloud has come.   We are proud of our
intellectual clouds; we like to travel in the
strength of them, to let men see that we are
influenced by them.   We make parade of our
doubt as if doubt were the symbol of plenty;
we forget that it is the sign of want.   Is there
not a better, a more excellent way ?   To thee,
as to all men, there must come moments of
darkness, moments when, like the Psalmist,
thou shalt cry, " Verily Thou art a God that
hidest Thyself."   But it is not well for thee

to *journey* in the darkness. It is not well for thee to go forth proclaiming to all the world that the shadows of an intellectual night have fallen upon thee, that truths once bright have become dim, that hopes once dear have become clouded. To-morrow the shades may all have passed away; morning may have come back to thy heart, and thy first faith may have risen in resurrection from the depths of night. And yet thy restoration may not restore the harm thou hast wrought on thy journey. What if thou hast affected others with thy clouds? what if thou hast impressed thy fellow-men with the gloom of thine own night? Their day may not come back when thy night shall vanish. Beware, therefore, O my soul, what thou shalt do under thy cloud. Beware that thou dost not journey while the shadow remains upon thee. Beware that thou dost not propagate in the hearts of others that which may only be transient in thine own. Be it thine to rest in secret while the cloud is hanging over thee, be it thine to tarry within while the shadow of doubt is overhead. One day thou shalt bless God that thou didst not journey, one day thou shalt rejoice that the cloud was kept secret in the depths of thy heart. For the cloud shall not be eternal. The sun of early hope shall rise, and the buds of early spring shall open, and the time for the singing of birds shall come, and then thou shalt be glad with an exceeding great joy. Thou shalt be glad that thou hast not revealed thy darkness, that thou hast not allowed the impressions of one misty hour to shade the eyes and disturb the thoughts of other men. When the cloud tarries upon thy tabernacle, keep the charge of the Lord and journey not.

XLIII.

THE VALUE OF PAIN.

" Yet it pleased the Lord to bruise Him ; . . . when Thou shalt make His soul an offering for sin, He shall see His seed, He shall prolong His days, and the pleasure of the Lord shall prosper in His hand."—ISA. liii. 10.

" IT pleased the Lord to bruise Him!" Strange pleasure this surely to dwell in the heart of the

All-Beneficent.   Is it not the nature of the heavenly Father to give joy? Does He not delight rather in the laughter than in the tears of men?   Why then should He find pleasure in the bruises of that heart in which there was no violence and no guile.   Nay, but look deeper. The prophet tells us that the bruises of the Servant of God were the source of His prosperity: "When Thou shalt make His soul an offering, He shall prolong His days."   Wherever the soul is offered, wherever the will is given, there is a fresh access of life.   Did not *He* find it so in the garden of Gethsemane? When did the angels come to Him with that strength which prolonged His days?   Was it not when He took the Father's cup in His hand and said, "Not as I will, but as Thou wilt."   No wonder that the Father was pleased to bruise Him; the bruising of His soul was the surrender of His will, and the surrender of His will was resurrection begun.   The pressure of the flower brought out its perfume; the breaking of the alabaster box diffused its fragrance till it filled all the house.   It recompensed the Father for the unloveliness of the past; it made atonement for the sins of the world.

Art thou chafing under the hand of thy God? art thou murmuring that He should seem to look on complacently while thy desire is being thwarted, while thy will is being denied? What if He *is* complacent? what if He is *pleased* to bruise thee? Thinkest thou that there cannot be a Divine benevolence which rejoices in thy moment of pain? Knowest thou not that there is a pain which gives cause for rejoicing? There is a pain which is the proof of convalescence, the sign that death is not yet. There is a pain which tells that the wound has not mortified, that there is life left in the mutilated member. There is a pain which is symptomatic of purity, which grows with the progress of purity, which cannot be felt by the impure. No conscience can feel the wound of sin but the tender conscience, no spirit can perceive its own unrest but the regenerated spirit. Ought not the sight of such pain to be dear to thy Father's heart? must not thy Father strive to produce such pain? What pleasure to Him can be the vision of thy perfect satisfaction with the earth; what is that but the vision that thou wert not made for Him. But if He shall see thee unsatisfied with the earth, if He shall make thee unsatisfied with the earth, then, indeed, it is meet that He should be glad, for, by the very want which earth cannot fill, He knows assuredly that thou art made for Himself alone. It is pleasing to thy Father's heart to see the travail of thy soul.

XLIV.

SPIRITUAL RESURRECTION.

" Son of man, can these bones live ?"—Ezek xxxvii. 3.

THERE are four degrees of wonderfulness in the Divine miracle of raising the dead. Some are like the daughter of Jairus; corruption has but begun when the arresting hand comes, and they revive. Some are like the youth of Nain; they are already on the road to burial when the mandate meets them, "Arise." Some are like Lazarus of Bethany; they are already in the grave, corruption is not merely begun, but almost perfected, when the summons is heard, "Come forth." There is one stage more wonderful still; it is that of Ezekiel's vision. There we seem to have reached the climax of impossibilities. It is not merely death that we see, it is not merely burial, it is not merely corruption begun, it is not merely corruption in its closing stage ; it is complete disintegration, it is the last result of decay. The bones are already scattered in the valley, and there is no sign remaining that they once had life. Could there be hope even for these? The prophet was doubtful, but He with whom he spake was not. There is more charity in the heart of God than in the heart of man. Finite love always despairs ; Infinite Love hopes boundlessly, unfathomably. It descends into the depths to seek and to save. It goes down to the valleys in search of the earth's rejected ones. It inquires for the lepers, the demoniacs, the Magdalenes whom the world has cast out. It weeps for those ruins of Jerusalem over which man rejoices, and its tears are not unprophetic of a redemptive hope.

My soul, never lose thy hope *in* the soul. However low it may have descended, however humiliating may be its valley, keep warm for it the fire of thy charity. Though it be already dead, though corruption be begun, though corruption be completed, though the last stage of disintegration be perfected, hope for it still. Let thy hope be the measure of thy love; where there is love there must be hope. It is not when thy vision is blackest that thy love is strongest. Art thou tempted to despair of humanity? Go and kindle thy devotion anew at the heart of Him who has borne its sins and carried its sorrows. Go and light thy torch at the glow of His life, who believed all things and hoped all things even whilst He endured all things. Then shalt thou despair no more, for in that glass of love wherein thou shalt behold His glory, thou shalt see His glory to be a ransomed soul.

XLV.

RELIGIOUS FEELING AND RELIGIOUS THOUGHT.

" *One thing have I desired of the Lord, that will I seek after ; that I may dwell in the house of the Lord all the days of my life, to behold the beauty of the Lord, and to inquire in His temple.*"—Ps. xxvii. 4.

THERE were two reasons why the Psalmist desired to dwell in the house of the Lord—he wanted to behold, and he wanted to inquire. Beholding and inquiring, the vision of the beauty and the study of the truth, make up together the perfect way. Without either of these our religion is a maimed religion. To behold the beauty without inquiring is mere sentiment, to inquire without beholding the beauty is mere criticism; perfect faith unites both. Yet there is an order in their union; the beholding of the beauty comes first. I cannot with any profit begin to inquire until I have begun to gaze; I cannot understand the reason until I have felt the power. Often have I marked these words of the Psalmist,

"O send out Thy light and Thy truth; let them lead me." He asks for the light before the truth; he desires the beauty before the knowledge. So have I ever felt that it must be with me. I would not pray for truth until I have prayed for light; I would not ask to inquire until I have learned to see. I feel that the house of my God is a house of mysteries. It has recesses which I cannot explore, it has secrets which I cannot fathom; but if I am allowed to gaze on its beauty I can afford to wait, if I am suffered to feel its splendour I can defer my right to search out its treasures.

O Thou who art fairer than the children of men, suffer me before all things to feast mine eyes on Thee. I may not be able any more than Nicodemus to assign the proof of Thy mission, but help me, unlike Nicodemus, to *see* the kingdom of God. Clouds and darkness are still round about my intellect, and my understanding can only cry, "O the depth;" but if Thou shalt open the eye of my heart I shall be independent of these. If Thou shalt suffer me to gaze on Thy beauty, I shall have

Thy light in anticipation of Thy truth, and in the strength of that light I shall go unto thine altar with exceeding joy. I would approach the problems of life with no other torch than thine ; be Thou Thine own interpreter, in Thy light let me see light. I shall both hear Thee and ask Thee questions when I have caught a vision of Thyself; when I have beheld Thy beauty I shall inquire in Thy tabernacle.

XLVI.

THE BLESSEDNESS OF DIVINE VISION.

" Blessed art thou, Simon Bar-jona: for flesh and blood hath not revealed it unto thee, but my Father which is in heaven."—MATT. xvi. 17.

THE Master is not here pronouncing a blessing on Peter ; He is declaring that Peter is already blessed. He is not promising him a place in the beatitudes of a future heaven ; He is proclaiming the truth that he has reached even now the heavenly beatific joy, " Blessed *art* thou." We speak of the dead as among the blessed, yet the living as well as the dead may reach the goal of blessedness. Why did the Master pronounce Peter blessed? It was because he had reached in life what is supposed to be the boon only of death—the joy of revelation. Is there to thee any blessedness equal to that, anything which thou wouldst choose in comparison with that? Hast thou too not felt at times the joy of a revelation which flesh and blood could never give, the rapture of seeing further than the bodily eye can see, of hearing further than the bodily ear can hear? When thou hast stood upon the margin of the shore and surveyed far and wide the expanse of waters, and when there has risen within thee a sense of the boundless, the infinite, the divine, what is that which has made thy blessedness? It is the knowledge that something has been revealed to thee which flesh and blood could not have revealed. What gave thee that sense of the boundless? Not the sea, for the sea was itself limited, and the finite cannot wake the infinite. It came from no material source; flesh and blood did not reveal it unto thee, but thy Father which is in heaven. That was the knowledge which made thee blessed in beholding the expanse of waters—the knowledge that thou wert larger than they. Yea, and that blessedness should be thine always, everywhere. For, indeed, thou art larger than all materialisms, O my soul. Flesh and blood could never have re-revealed to thee any of the things which make thee man. Even the visible form of the Christ would not have revealed to thee His beauty ; if thou hast seen His beauty, it is by another eye than sense. If thy heart has burned as He talked with thee by the way, if thine aspiration has soared as He pointed thee to the mount of God, it can only be because thy heart is already one with His heart, because thine aspiration is already harmonious with His holy will. Thou couldst not have seen Him as He is if thou hadst not been like Him, for the divine alone can recognise the divine. The mutual recognition is the proof of a kindred spirit : " Blessed art thou."

XLVII.

THE IMMEDIATE VISION OF GOD.

" *If there be a prophet among you, I the Lord will make myself known unto him in a vision, and will speak unto him in a dream. My servant Moses is not so, who is faithful in all mine house. With him will I speak mouth to mouth.*"—NUM. xii. 6–8.

THEY tell us that in the old days men were superstitious, that they could only see God in visions and in dreams. But in the oldest days of all it was not so. Here is a very ancient book which makes the visions and the dreams the marks not of a higher, but of a lower revelation. We are apt to think that the most privileged men of the Bible were the men who had visions; here the reverse is assumed. It is taken for granted that Moses was more privileged than others just because he had no visions. The ordinary prophet saw God only in the symbol; Moses was rewarded for his fidelity by seeing no symbol, beholding no vision, receiving no dream, but by speaking with God in the light of open day.

For me, too, there is deep meaning in these words of the ancient book. Often have I complained within myself that my life has fallen on evil days. Often have I longed to get back to the times of miracle, of vision, and of dream, and have held those to be specially favoured who were thus permitted to commune with God. Yet the judgment of these times themselves was very different; it prized more the lot which has fallen to me. It held those to be the least favoured who did not see God face to face, nor speak with Him mouth to mouth, but who beheld Him only through the miraculous cloud and fire. Therefore, my soul, weep not for the miraculous messengers, for the pillar of cloud by day, and the pillar of fire by night. Thine is a higher privilege than to see God through intermediaries; thou canst see Him for thyself. The messengers are withdrawn, but only because the King himself has come. What need for thee to hear voices in the night, when by night and day thou hast one per-

petual voice? What need for thee to see
special visions, when all sense is one con-
tinuous vision — the vision of His divine
garment as His presence passes by? What
need for thee to receive at intervals the falling
manna, when thou canst partake every hour
and every moment of that gift of natural
beneficence—the old corn of the land?

XLVIII.

THE KEY TO GOD'S SILENCE.

" We shall all be changed."—1 COR. xv. 51.

OFTEN have I asked myself, Why is it that
the religion of the Son of Man is so silent
about the destiny of the sons of men? He
has told us of many mansions, but He has not
revealed their form. Other masters have been
explicit, minute, detailed in their descriptions
of the coming heaven, but the verdict even of
Christ's most beloved disciple is this: "It
doth not yet appear what we shall be." And

H

here is the key to the whole silence : before we
reach heaven " we shall all be changed." It
is as if it were said : What is the use of
describing the joys of heaven ? they would
not be joys to you as yet. You would not
tell the child of the pleasures he shall have
when he becomes a man. And why ? because
the pleasantness of these pleasures is now
beyond him. He would shed bitter tears to
be told that in the time to come he should
rejoice in that which is not play—in study, in
work, in care, in responsibility, in duty. He
shall see the glory of these things when he
himself shall be changed.

Thou who art crying for a new revelation of
heaven, art thou ready for thy wish ? Would
it be to thee a joy if there were revealed to thee
the pleasures at God's right hand ? What if
these pleasures should be what the selfish man
calls pain ? Knowest thou not that the joys of
love are not the joys of lovelessness ? Love's
joy is the surrender of itself; the joy of lovelessness is the keeping of itself. If heaven
were open to thy vision, the sight might startle
thee ; thou mightst call for the rocks to hide

thee, for the mountains to cover thee from the view. To make the revelation a joy to thee thou thyself must be changed into the same image. It is not every soul that can rejoice to be a ministering spirit sent forth to minister to the heirs of salvation ; to rejoice in it fully we must all be changed. If death were abolished to-day it would not free thee from that need. It is not death that demands thy change ; it is life. It is not death that brings thy change; it is the Spirit of the Christ. Thou needst not wait for death to find thy change, for the Spirit too can transform in a moment, in the twinkling of an eye. Blessed are they who shall not taste of death until they shall see the kingdom of God.

XLIX.

PEACE BETTER THAN JOY.

" Son, thou art ever with me, and all that I have is thine."—LUKE xv. 31.

THE elder brother was surprised at the prodigal's joy, surprised that such a joy should have been vouchsafed to him. He saw him in the experience of a rapture which he himself had never possessed and could not now command, and it seemed for the time an incongruous thing. He had lived all his life in his father's house, and had never strayed from the haunts of home, yet he had never known the ecstasy of the human spirit; his brother had only now wakened to the thought of home, and his heart was on fire with joy. Was the elder son inferior by reason of this greater calm? Not so thought the Father. "Son, thou art ever with me, and all that I have is thine." To Him the greater calm was a proof of greater nearness. It was just because there had been no interruption in the home-life that there was no place for ecstasy. This man had never seen aught but beauty, never heard aught but music; wherefore should he cry out in rapture at a scene or break forth into ecstasy at a song? God's breath was in him every moment, every hour, every day; why should he be excited by that which to him was no new thing? Verily, peace was from him a higher tribute than joy.

My soul, do not undervalue thy peace. Do not say that the calm that has never left a Father's house is inferior to the flutter that has waked in coming home. It is not inferior, it is brighter, purer. He who has gone forth into the far country and wasted his substance in riotous living may in his return experience a joy of contrast which others cannot know, for the transition from midnight into day must indeed be dazzling, radiant. Yet methinks it is better to have the day without the night, the home without the exile, the calm without the storm. There may be less joy, but there will be more peace; there will be less marvel, but there will be more permanence. To breathe the breath of God as a natural atmosphere—that is the highest blessing, and the highest tribute of Infinite Love is this: " Son, thou art ever with me, and all that I have is thine."

L.

OBEDIENCE BETTER THAN SACRIFICE.

"Behold, to obey is better than sacrifice."—1 SAM. xv. 22.

WHEN Samuel spoke these words he was a Christian. In that moment he had leapt the gulf of centuries, and left his nation far behind. He had caught the glimmer of a new and better sun—the Light that waited to lighten every man. Well might he cry to his countrymen, "Behold!" for the thing he was about to utter was to them a startling thing. They had thought that the crown of religion was sacrifice, pain, the sense of privation and suffering; he tells them that the crown of religion is the abolition of the sense of pain, the overcoming of the feeling of privation. He tells them that the crown of religion is to obey, to yield the will, to surrender the life, to have a heart harmonious with the thing commanded. Not the pain but the painlessness was the glory, not the suffering involved in the doing, but the delight with which the work was done ; to obey was better than sacrifice.

O Thou that desirest not sacrifice, that seekest not the pain but the glory of Thy people,
let me enter into Thy joy—the joy of my
Lord. Let me enter into that joy whose
delight was to do Thy will, into that rest that
under the shadow of a cross could say, "Peace
I leave with you; my peace I give unto you."
Let me be dead to the law through His spirit
of universal love; let the sense of duty itself
be transcended in the thought of glorious privilege. There is no pain in love any more
than there is fear. Why should I measure my
piety by my misery? why should grace be
high when the temperature of nature is low?
It is not my penance that brings me near to
Thee; it is my penance that proves me to be
still distant from Thee. When I shall touch
Thee there shall be no more penance, no more
night, no more sea, no more sacrifice. I shall
have reached that perfect obedience which is
perfect love, and therefore perfect painlessness. The chains shall fall from me, the
clouds shall melt from me, the shadows shall
fly from me, and in the spirit of Him who has
conquered not only death but sacrifice, I too

shall be able to say, " Lo, I come ; I delight to do Thy will."

LI.

THE CURE FOR PAIN.

" And Elijah said unto her, Fear not ; go and do as thou hast said : but make me thereof a little cake first, and bring it unto me, and after make for thee and for thy son."—1 KINGS xvii. 13.

A WONDERFULLY suggestive picture ! The prophet of God brings to a starving woman the revelation of coming plenty, and He tells her to work on the faith of its coming. But strange to say, she is to begin her work not by getting but by giving. Her first gathering is to be not for herself but for another—for the prophet of God : " Make me a little cake first, and after make for thee and for thy son." Do not wonder at such a command. Do not think that it implied any coldness in the heart of the prophet, any indifference to human want, any ignorance of the pains of poverty.

It was a command sublimely benevolent, far-reaching in its appreciation of the needs of man. Is not our first need, whether in things spiritual or things temporal, to be lifted out of ourselves? Self-thought is the deepest source of our pain. Am I oppressed with the burden and heat of the day? it will do me no good to dwell upon it, it will only be increased by meditation. Let me remember that other souls are also weighed down by the same burden and the same heat, that other hearts are also heavy with a like labour and laden-ness. If I can remember this, my own burden shall fall from me; if I can give first to others I shall be strong to procure for myself. Therefore, my soul, there is for thee a deep meaning in this picture. Art thou in trouble? others are in trouble. Art thou in bereavement? there is not a house without its vacant chair. Art thou perplexed with mystery? thou hast a *fellowship* in the mystery. Hast thou no thought for those who suffer what thou sufferest? arise and look around thee. There are hearts to be bound like thine, there are tears to be dried like thine, there are days to be illumined like thine. Thy very sorrow has put a gift into thy hand—sympathy. Give it, and the store of thine own strength shall be increased. Go forth from thyself but for an hour, and verily on thy return thou shalt find the old place radiant with a new light, beautiful with a new glory, holy with a new spirit—the Spirit of the Lord.

LII.

GOD'S PROMISE OF PROSPERITY.

" Whatsoever he doeth shall prosper."—Ps. i. 3.

Our first thought is, what a grand promise, what an incentive to the good man to *be* good ! Who would not be a saint to have such purple and fine linen and sumptuous faring every day, to have a passport through the world to fortune, to be promised that in all things he should prosper? Our second thought is, is it true? Do we see that the saint prospers in whatsoever he doeth? Does it not rather seem as if the man of God were the man of special burdens, labouring more than others, heavy laden above his fellows. Our third thought is, have we rightly *read* the promise? Does it mean what we have taken it to mean? Is it really said that the good man shall prosper in whatsoever he doeth? Nay, but something very different is said, "Whatsoever he doeth shall prosper." The Psalmist is not thinking of the man, but of the work. The prosperity which he promises is not the earthly triumph of the individual, but the earthly triumph of the truth which he proclaims. The man himself may die ere his work be done. Moses may sink weary by the wayside and the commonplace Joshua in his room may enter in, but his work shall not die, it shall be found again after many days: "Whatsoever he doeth shall prosper."

Does this seem to thee a less glorious reading of the promise? If thou art a man of God it cannot do so. To the man of God there is nothing so dear as the work of God. No promise would to him be so sweet as the prosperity of that work, not even the promise of his own prosperity. Art thou dearer to thyself than thy work ? then thou art not yet fit to be a worker. If thou shalt stand on Mount Nebo and behold the Promised Land of thine own labours which yet thou thyself shalt never reach, wilt thou weep because Joshua shall enter in ? If so, it shall not be written of thee, "His eye was not dim, nor his natural strength abated." But if the spirit of Christ be thine, if thou shalt merge thyself in thy labour, if thou shalt lose thyself in the glory of thy mission, thine is, indeed, a vision undimmed. Thou shalt see of the travail of thy soul and shalt be satisfied— satisfied because others shall reap in joy what thou hast sown in tears. Thy surest word of prophecy shall be thy highest source of blessing : " Whatsoever he doeth shall prosper."

LIII.

SIN'S FIRST MANIFESTATION.

"And he sent them to Bethlehem, and said, Go and search diligently for the young child ; and when ye have found Him, bring me word again, that I may come and worship Him also."—MATT. ii. 6.

THERE it is. Sin never reveals itself at the outset *as* sin ; if it did, we should at once be repelled. If it came to the youth and said, " I am evil ; follow me," is there any youth in the nation who would obey it ? The spell is broken when Satan declares himself to *be* Satan, when he says in so many words, " Fall down and worship me." But when the tempter first comes to the soul he comes not in his own dress ; he comes in the dress of virtue. So far from appearing as the solicitor to evil, he professes to be the ally of what is good and true. He proclaims not himself as the enemy of the Christ, but as one who would support and further the cause of Christ. The allurement of vice is its resemblance to virtue ;

it adorns itself in borrowed robes. It assumes
the counterfeit of that freedom which belongs
only to the Spirit of the Master. It bids the
youth say, "I do not care," in counterfeit of
that divine carelessness which has cast its burdens on the Lord. It offers him a prospect
of self-abandonment in counterfeit of the
Christian self-surrender. It tells him to break
the shackles of authority and come out into
the open plain, in counterfeit of that holier
consciousness, "I am dead to the law that I
might live unto God."

My soul, distrust the seeming resemblances
between the kingdom of Herod and the kingdom of Christ. There is not, there never can
be, an alliance between them ; their likeness
lies on the surface. License is not freedom ;
libertinism is not liberty ; recklessness is not
conquest of care ; self-will is not manliness.
Go and search diligently for the young child,
and when thou hast found Him, thou wilt
find that Herod could never have worshipped
Him. Their unlikeness will grow the longer
they stand side by side. Herod asks from
thee at the beginning only a trifling tribute,

but he concludes by proving thee a slave; Christ at the outset demands thy heart, thy strength, thine all, but He ends by making thee free. It is not Herod, but the star of unselfish hope that can lead thee to the place where the young Child lies.

LIV.

HOW TO KNOW GOD'S LOVE.

" To know the love of Chris', which passeth knowledge."—
EPH. iii. 19.

Do not say within thyself, I will not believe what I do not understand. There is a faculty in thee that passeth understanding. Thou hast a power which is higher than reason, and which sees what reason cannot see. Thy reason can only mount on the steps of an argument, but there is something in thee which flies to truth's conclusion as the lark flies to the morning. Thou canst not weigh it, thou canst not measure it, thou canst not with accuracy even name it, yet it lifts thee into regions beyond thine understanding, it carries thee into worlds which transcend thy reason, it passeth the powers of knowledge.

There are two things which pass thy knowledge in the sphere of faith, two things which thou canst not know by the understanding— the peace of Christ and the love of Christ. All reason would say that their existence is impossible. How can a man have peace when the waters are swelling round him? how can a man be divinely loved ere he is yet divinely lovely? Yet the peace and the love alike come through shut doors; how they come we cannot tell, yet we feel that they are here. Thou knowest it is *His* peace by thy calm in storm; unrest could never have created rest. Thou knowest it is *His* love by thy want in affluence; the earth and the fulness thereof could never have made thy thirst for heaven. It is by thy longing for Him thou knowest that He longeth for thee. Thou couldst not have panted for Him if He had not panted for thee. Thy love for Him is to His love for thee what the sunlight on the sea is to the sunshine in the sky—a reflex, a mirror, a diffusion ; thou art giving back the glory that has been cast upon the waters. In the attraction of thy life to Him, in the cleaving of thy heart to Him, in the soaring of thy spirit to Him, thou art told that He is near thee. In all that thou hast done and thought and suffered for His sake, in all that thou hast purposed and planned and achieved for His service, in every movement wherewith thy spirit has vibrated at the sound of His name, thou hearest the beating of His pulse for thee, thou knowest that He loves thee.

LV.

THE BOLDNESS OF CHRISTIAN HOPE.

" That ye might be filled with all the fulness of God."— Eph. iii. 19.

WHAT an aspiration for a band of fishermen, peasants, slaves ! It was an aspiration after

more than Roman dominion, after more than
Judaic empire. The proudest dreams of Pan-
theism never dared to soar so high. The
Brahman had aspired to be lost in God, to
have the little spark of his individual being
absorbed in the mighty fire of the universe;
that was rather humility than pride. Here
was a company of men aspiring to reach God
yet not to be lost in God, aiming to touch the
brightness of the Infinite Glory without losing
the spark of their own individual being. Was
not this presumption, was not this impiety,
was not this fitted to destroy all the tender
graces of the Christian life?—the poverty of
spirit which had been promised the kingdom,
the meekness of heart which was to inherit the
earth. ;

Nay, but who *was* this God with whose
fulness they desired to be filled? His name
was Love. If His name had been aught else
than Love the desire of these men would have
been indeed presumption. But to be filled
with the fulness of love is not pride; it is the
deepest, the most intense humility. He that
is filled with love is thereby made the servant

of all; he repeats the life of the Divine Man, and becomes heir to His burden. To him belong sorrows not his own. He labours in the labour of humanity, he suffers in the tears of affliction, he is wounded in the battle of the weak. His glory is his pain. That which fills him with God is that which fills him with sadness, which bows him down with the sense of nothingness; the love that makes him great is the power that makes him gentle. O Love that passest knowledge, come into my heart with all Thy fulness, that my heart may be made gentle with Thy gentleness. Without Thee I have no humility, because I have no burden; I live for myself, because I have no thought beyond self. But when Thou shalt enter in I shall cease to be my own. I shall become heir to the sins and sorrows of the vast world, I shall take up the crosses of the labouring and the heavy-laden. When I am filled by *Thee* I shall be emptied of all pride; when I am conscious of Thee I shall be forgetful of myself. In Thy strength shall I find my weakness, in Thy wealth shall I learn my poverty, in Thy fulness shall I awake to the

sense of my nothingness; I shall become the
servant of humanity when Thou shalt fill my
soul.

————————

LVI.

SPIRITUAL WEANING.

" When the unclean spirit is gone out of a man, he walketh
through dry places, seeking rest, and findeth none."—
MATT. xii. 43.

THERE is no moment of the spiritual life so
painful and so dangerous as its weaning; the
old is past, and the new is not yet come. The
hardest time to bear is neither Egypt nor the
Promised Land, but the desert that lies between. Egypt has the pleasures of sin, the
Promised Land has the pleasures of holiness,
but the desert has no pleasures. It has given
up the joys of Pharaoh, and it has not yet
reached the delights of Canaan. It is only a
stage of prohibitions; it forbids the pleasures
of the past, and it has as yet not even the
grapes of Eshcol to offer in their room.

My soul, thou canst not rest in the desert,
thou canst not be satisfied with a law which
only says, "Thou shalt not." It is a hard
thing to have the old cup snatched from thy
lips ere any new cup is presented to thee. It
is a hard thing to have the old tenants ex-
pelled from thy dwelling ere any new guests
are admitted there. It is a hard thing to
have the house empty, swept, and garnished
ere ever thou hast learned that it is empty
for the reception of new visitors, garnished for
the coming of nobler guests. Thine old love
of sin cannot be replaced by law; it can only
be replaced by a new love. Thine old joy in
Egypt cannot be supplanted by fear; it can
only be supplanted by the joy of Canaan. It
is vain to tell thee to walk not in the counsel
of the ungodly, and stand not in the way of
sinners, until thy *delight* shall be in the law of
the Lord and thy meditation on it day and
night. Therefore thy prayer must be: O
Love that art the recompense for every loss,
send into my heart the well-spring of Thy joy,
to gladden with its healing waters the places
that have been left dry. Fill up the solitudes

of that spirit which has been emptied of its old treasures and swept of its past ideals. Teach me that behind the reproach of the desert there is to be found greater riches than all the treasures of Egypt. Change the struggle of my dawn into the spontaneity of a second day. Let law become grace ; let duty become privilege ; let service become freedom ; let work become play ; let sacrifice become joy. When I shall exchange the spirit of heaviness for the garment of praise, the old house shall be empty no more.

LVII.

THE UNIVERSAL HARMONY.

" And I looked, and, lo, a Lamb stood on the mount Sion, and with Him an hundred forty and four thousand, having His Father's name written in their foreheads. . . . And I heard the voice of harpers harping with their harps."—REV. xiv. 1-2.

THE summing up of the universe is the revelation of harmony. It is not that the harmony

comes at the end, but that the harmony is revealed at the end. The universe is all music,
but it is not all music to our ear. We only
hear a few chords, and they are minor chords.
The minor chords seem discords when they
stand alone ; they want the full symphony to
bring out their symmetry. Often art thou
crying out that thou art living in a world of
discords. Thou art living in a world of perfect
music, only thou hearest but a small portion
of the music. Often art thou saying that the
coming melody shall atone for the jarring
chords. Nay; say rather that the jarring
chords themselves shall be revealed as parts
of the completed harmony. The melody is
not to come, it has come already ; it has only
to be completed to be revealed, and then the
harpers shall stand upon the glassy sea.

My soul, bethink thee, what *was* that
which to the Seer of Patmos made the harmony complete? It was the vision of a vast
multitude surrounding with their praises the
Lamb of sacrifice. There was a time when, to
that multitude, the spectacle of sacrifice would
have brought discord to the heart; in the

completed harmony it brings joy. The sweetest music to the heart of thy God is the ripeness of thy soul for sacrifice, the moment when thou art able to say, "I am now ready to be offered." At such a moment all the sorrows of life are justified, sanctified. The minor chords get a meaning and receive a vindication when the harpers stand around Mount Zion in praise of the sacrificial Lamb. Knowest thou not that this was from the outset the goal of thy being—to be made perfect through suffering? It was for this that thy first innocence was clouded. It was for this that thy first joy was dimmed. It was for this that thy first hope was shaken—that thou mightest reach Olivet by the steps of Calvary. The wilderness of the Son of Man is better than the garden of Adam. The morning stars sang together over thine untried nature; but there awaits thee a yet grander music—when the harps of God shall proclaim that thou hast conquered through the Cross.

LVIII.

CHRISTIANITY NOT ASCETICISM.

*" But if we walk in the light, as He is in the light, we have
fellowship one with another."*—1 JOHN i. 7.

" IF we walk in the light we have fellowship."
What a difference between the Divine and the
human view of religion! Most of us are
saying within our hearts, "If we walk in the
light, we ought to have no fellowship." I once
thought that religion meant withdrawal from
the haunts of men. I thought that it signified
separation, isolation, asceticism, penance, joy-
lessness; I thought that the light manifested
itself by darkness. God says, on the contrary,
that life never becomes social until His light
has come. It is the want of His light that
prevents me from having fellowship, that
debars me from enjoying companionship. As
long as my heart is dark I will not reveal it
to my brother-man; as long as his heart is
dark he will not reveal it to me. And so
we are both alone. Our solitude is the fruit

of our darkness; if the light would come we would have fellowship. All light pants to reveal itself. Who ever sought fellowship like *Him*—the light and life of men? To whom did He not outpour Himself? to whom did He not reveal Himself? What sphere of human history did He not strive to make His own? Pharisee and publican, Jew and Gentile, rich and destitute, learned and ignorant—He met them all. He touched those spheres of worldliness which the world itself could not touch without increased defilement. He was the light, and therefore He could touch the darkness. O light that lightest every man, come into this heart of mine that in Thy radiance I may have Thy power of fellowship. I am weary of my own narrowness, I am tired of my own isolation; I long to be able like Thee to break through the limits that debar me from the life of my brother. I long to be able like Thee to touch impurity without stain, to shine in darkness without receiving its shadow. I long like Thee to sympathise with that which is beneath me, to love that which is unlike me, to commune with that which has no voice for me. Only in Thee shall that power be mine, therefore I wait for Thy coming. When Thou shalt touch me with Thy presence, I too shall touch all things. I shall pass uncorrupted into the scenes of this great world. I shall mingle in its pursuits and they shall not hurt me, I shall join in its pleasures and they will not harm me, I shall study its aims and they will not lower my heavenly aspiration, I shall meet with its prodigal children and my garments shall be undefiled; all fellowship shall be mine when I walk in Thy light.

LIX.

CHRISTIAN CHARITY.

" Add to brotherly kindness charity."—2 PET. i. 7.

CHRISTIANITY here reveals itself as the religion of universal love. It tells men that it is not enough for them to be kind to those who are their *brethren;* they must be kind to those who are not their brethren. It is not enough for them to love those that are at one with them; they must love those that are not at one with them. Christ's love is like no other love; it goes down to those that are outside the pale of loveliness. Human love can only seek her own, can only love that which is like herself. Man seeks fellowship with him that has a kindred soul. He goes out to meet the heart that is already in sympathy with his heart, he gives back to his brother what his brother has given to him. But Divine love transcends the limits of its own sympathies. It seeks those that are not yet brethren; it goes forth to *make* brotherhood. It keeps not on the plain of its own being; it descends into the valleys to seek and to save that which is lost. It travels down into the depths to bring up that which as yet has no affinity to itself. It follows the prodigals afar off, it searches out the lepers amid the tombs, it gathers in the outcasts from the highways and the hedges; it seeks those who are not beautiful, that it may endow them with its beauty.

O Thou Divine Love, that hast revealed to me the infinite possibilities of loving, make me a sharer in Thy life. Much of what I call my love is but disguised selfishness. I seek others because I find myself in them. My heart goes out to the hearts that go out to me, my sympathy expands to the sympathies that agree with me, my kindness is but *brotherly* kindness. I want more than that. I want kindness for the unbrotherly, sympathy for the erring, tenderness for the fallen, love for the lost. In Thee, in Thee alone shall I find them. Breathe into my heart the breath of Thine own life, that my life may no longer be my own. Inspire me with the glory of Thy Cross—the joy of bearing the burdens of the world's weak ones. Lay upon me that yoke of Thine which is easy because it kills all selfish care—the yoke of humanity, the care for other souls. Then shall my heart be enlarged to meet the life of man. Then in the depth of Thy love shall I go down into the depths of humanity, and shall claim my brotherhood with every human soul. When I have reached the power of universal charity I shall be made divine in Thee.

The power of universal charity

LX.

CHRIST'S SENSE OF MYSTERY.

" He marvelled because of their unbelief."—MARK vi. 6.

THE acts of the Son of Man are to us miraculous; we marvel at His deeds. But have we
ever thought that our acts were to *Him*
miraculous ? He marvelled at us as much
as we marvelled at Him. True, the cause of
the wonder was in each case different. *We*
wondered at His greatness ; He wondered at
our littleness. Everything is a miracle when
it transcends the law of our nature. Our
littleness transcended the law of *His* nature.
He could not understand our meanness of
heart, our selfishness of aim, our coldness of
affection, our absence of enthusiasm, our dim-
ness of faith ; He marvelled at it. It was all
so unlike *Him*, that to Him it was a miracle.
He saw in it a violation of the law of Divine
nature, a suspension of the powers resident in
the heaven-born soul. He beheld in it a

greater transformation than we beheld in the
turning of water into wine; that was but the
transforming of matter into matter, this was the
turning of life into death. It was the earthli-
ness of that which should be heavenly, the
meanness of that which should be majestic,
the poverty of that which should be precious,
the deadness of that which should be alive for
evermore; it contradicted the whole range of
His Divine experience, and He marvelled with
an exceeding great surprise.

My soul, be not thou a miracle to thy Lord.
Be not thou a thing at which He that fashioned
thee shall wonder. Be not thou so unlike
His nature as to seem to Him a prodigy, an
object at which to gaze and marvel. Rather
be it thine to enter into union with His
infinite order, to be harmonious with His
eternal law. Be it thine to catch so much of
His likeness that He shall recognise Himself
in thee, shall behold as in a glass His own
glory, shall rejoice at the sight of that which
is familiar to Him. Then shall He wonder at
thee no more, for He shall find in thee a
kindred life. He shall see in thee the reflex

of His own light, the shadow of His own form, the travail of His own soul. He shall behold in thee what the Father has beheld in Him—the brightness of His glory and the express image of His person.

———

LXI.

THE KNOCKING OF THE SPIRIT.

" Behold, I stand at the door and knock."—Rev. iii. 20.

WHY does He not come in ? Is not this Divine Spirit omnipotent ? Has He not power to enter where He will, to breathe where He chooses, to blow where He listeth ? Why, then, does He stand without, knocking at the door of a frail human heart ? Could He not break down that door in a moment, in the twinkling of an eye, and annihilate that opposing barrier which disputes His claim to universal empire ? Yes, but in so doing He would annihilate also the man. What makes me a man is just my power to open the door.

If I had no power to open or to forbear opening I would not be responsible. The Divine
Spirit might then, indeed, do with me what
He will, but I would not be worth His possession. I would be simply as the unconscious stars which He fills with light, as the
blind winds which He directs on their way.
But if the stars and the winds had been
enough He would never have said, "Let us
make man." He made me because He meant
me to be more than a star, more than a breath
of heaven. He meant me to respond to Himself, to open on His knocking at the door.
He could have no joy in breaking down the
door, in taking the kingdom of my heart by
violence; there would be no response in that,
no answer of a heart to His heart, no accept-
ance of a will by His will. Therefore, He
prefers to stand without till I open, to knock
till I hear, to speak till I respond. He would
not have my being to be lost in His, for His
being is love, and love demands love.

O Thou Divine Spirit, that in all events of
life art knocking at the door of my heart, help
me to respond to Thee. I would not be

K

driven blindly as the stars over their courses. I would not be made to work out Thy will unwillingly, to fulfil Thy law unintelligently, to obey Thy mandates unsympathetically. Where Thou goest I would go, where Thou dwellest I would dwell. I would take the events of my life as good and perfect gifts from Thee; I would receive even the sorrows of life as disguised gifts from Thee. I would have my heart open at all times to receive Thee—at morning, noon, and night; in spring, and summer, and winter. Whether Thou comest to me in sunshine or in rain, I would take Thee into my heart joyfully. Thou art Thyself more than the sunshine, Thou art Thyself compensation for the rain; it is Thee and not Thy gifts I crave; knock and I shall open unto Thee.

LXII.

MOMENTS OF ANTICIPATION.

" And Jesus saith unto him, I will come and heal him."—
Matt. viii. 7.

THERE are some prayers which are answered
only by the promise of an answer. The cen-
turion prays for his servant that he may be
healed instantaneously; the immediate response is, I *will* come. Have you and I never
experienced this? We have asked something
which has not at once been granted, and yet
we have been made to feel that there was
something more than silence. We have felt
in our hearts what seemed the prophecy of
an answer, a nameless, unspeakable strength
which told us it would one day all be well.
The summer did not come immediately, but the
swallows came into our spring, and the interpre-
tation of their song was this, "It will come."

My soul, do not despise thy moments of
anticipation. They have no present gifts to
bring, but they bring the promise of great gifts

to come; they have no immediate answer to thy prayer, but they tell thee of a time when thy prayer *will* be answered. Thinkest thou it is a light thing to have such moments? Great men have lived on them and died on them. Did not Abraham leave his country and his father's house with no other food in his heart than the strength of a promise? Was it not that promise that helped him to climb the Mount Moriahs of life, and to meet on their summits the great sacrifices to which life is heir; he was made strong by the power of aspiration, by the voice which each morning said to him, "I will come." So shalt thou too be strong, O my soul. If thou shalt set out on thy journey with the prophecy of an answered prayer, thou too shalt climb Mount Moriah with unfaltering feet, thou too with unblanched cheek shalt meet the sacrifice on its summit. The glory of to-morrow shall prefigure itself through the tears of to-day, and the song of the approaching swallows shall be heard amid the snow; all shadows vanish from that heart to which God has said, "I will come."

LXIII.

WAYSIDE SEEDS.

"*Some seeds fell by the wayside.*"—MATT. xiii. 4.

THERE are some men who have no experience, only *experiences*. They never gain any lesson from life itself, only from what they call the startling *events* of life. They are stirred into emotion by what seem to them the accidents of the world. When death comes suddenly and unexpectedly they are impressed with solemnity, they are religious for an hour; but the seed has fallen only by the wayside. My soul, is it so with thee? Art thou living simply by the *wayside* of life? Art thou waking up at stray moments to the conviction that there are solemnities in this life of thine? Art thou living in indifference between the falling of each new seed? Art thou only awakened by what thou callest the catastrophes of life—by death, by war, by commercial panic? Then thou art only catching seeds by the wayside. Yet the way is more solemn than the wayside. No event of thy life is half so startling, half so awful, half so mysterious as thy life itself. Nothing that happens to thee is so worthy of meditation as thine own being. The seeds that fall by the wayside are less important than the intervening space that lies between. The quiet time when there is nothing startling is the most eventful time of all, for it is then that thou thyself art growing—growing by the nourishment of the past seed, and ripening for nourishment by the seed which is to come.

How shall I reach this sense of solemnity, of solemnity everywhere and always? Lord, I can only reach it in Thee. If I felt, like the Psalmist, that Thou wert continually with me, I would feel continually solemn. It is because I feel Thee to be with me only at startling moments that I lose the sense of life's universal solemnity. Therefore, Thou all-pervading Divine Spirit, do Thou impress me with Thine all-pervadingness. Teach me that Thou art not in one place more than another. Teach me that I cannot flee from Thy presence, that Thou art with me not only in the Bethanies and the Calvaries, but in the common toil of Nazareth, and in the silent solitudes of the wilderness. So, in the sense of Thy continual presence, shall my way be uniformly great, and the events of the wayside shall be startling no more. All life shall be alike solemn when I have learned that I am ever with Thee. I shall cease to live by the impressions of the hour when every breath of my being comes to me as a gift Divine.

LXIV.

HUMAN UNREST.

"As the hart panteth after the water brooks, so panteth my soul after Thee, O God."—Ps. xlii. 1.

ALL things live in their own element—the cattle on the plain, the fish in the sea, the bird in the air. Thy element is God. Thou art the only creature in this universe that art not now *in* thine element; thou art an anomaly in the order of creation. The sparrow hath an house and the swallow a nest for herself, but thou longest, faintest; thou hast not found a resting-place in all the tabernacles of time. Thou art the least happy of all creatures. The bird carols in the air all the day, but thou hast not a day quite undimmed by tears. Why is it thus with thee? Wherefore art thou less happy than the beast of the field? Is it because thou hast fewer resources? Nay, it is because thy resources are greater, because they are too great for the world that environs thee. It is because thou art not living in thine element, and the element in which thou livest is not adequate to thy powers. Thou hast capacities for boundless flight, and thou art chained within a limited area; thou art made for God, and thou art narrowed to the dust. No wonder thou art not happy; it is thy greatness makes thee unhappy. If thou hadst been a bird of the air thou wouldst have carolled like him, but because thou art more thou hast no unclouded song. And yet thou wert made for song. Thou wert not only made for song in a future vorld, thou wert designed for it here. Thou art promising thyself joy in regions beyond the grave, but the only element that can give thee joy is on both sides of the grave. Thy joy is God, and God is here as well as there. The atmosphere of the Divine surrounds thee *now*. Thou needst not wait for death to reach it; thou canst soar into it at any moment. Say not that others have their portion here, but that thou hast thy portion hereafter; is not thy portion eternity, and is not eternity now as well as then? Thy portion is here, my soul,—on the threshold of thy life, at the door of thy being; it is *in* the earth, though it is not of the earth. Why shouldst thou pant any more? The river that makes glad the city of God can make glad the cities of men. Thou canst find thine element as easily as the hart findeth the water brooks. "Ho, every one that thirsteth, come ye to the waters."

LXV.

THE FIGHT OF FAITH.

" By little and little I will drive them out from before thee."—Exod. xxiii. 30.

Is my life, then, to be a perpetual warfare ? Is it only by little and little that I am to con- quer my spiritual foes ? I thought that in coming to Christ I was coming to the end of struggle ; did He not say, " Come unto me all ye that labour, and I will give you rest " ? Yet here it would seem as if the coming to Him were the promise of war. Yes, but the two promises do not contradict each other. The rest which He offers thee is a rest not *from* struggle but *in* struggle. He has a higher gift for thee than the mere cessation from life's battle : His gift to thee is the power to fight. Knowest thou not that the first fruit of the Divine life within thee is the sense of struggle and the power of struggle. There is no warfare in spiritual death any more than in natural death ; it is the calm of the sepulchre. But the rest of God comes to break the calm of the sepulchre. The rest of God is love, and love is labour. Perfect love is perfect power of labouring; completed love is complete strength for ladenness. Thy struggle is itself thy victory. Hast thou pondered the meaning of these words of Paul, " In all these thing we are more than conquerors " ? What things is he speaking of ? " Tribulation, distress, persecution, famine, nakedness, peril, sword." Should we not have expected him to have said, " *Over* all these things we are more than conquerors " ? Yes, had he meant to say so ; but that was not the thought in his mind. Paul was not thinking of how we should get rid of tribulation and persecution, but of how tribulation and persecution would make us strong. It was not the freedom from the struggle, but the moral exercise of the struggle that caused his heart to triumph ; therefore he was not afraid to say, " *In* all these things we are conquerors." " Blessed are they that are persecuted," says a greater than Paul. Why does He close the beatitudes with such a blessing as this ? Just because it is the fitting

crown of all.   It is much to be poor in spirit,
to be meek, to be merciful, to be peaceable,
to be pure in heart—but to be all these things
through struggle, this is holiness indeed. Therefore *by little and little* God will drive out thy
foes.   He will not rob thee of the moral health
of struggle by granting thee a sudden triumph.
Day by day He shall renew the exercise of
thy patience, the trial of thy faith, the proof
of thy love, the test of thy temper, the train-
ing of thy will.   Day by day He shall grant
thee a fresh field to conquer, a new victory
to win, till in the calm of conscious strength
thou shalt be able to say, " Thou preparest
a table before me in the presence of mine
enemies."

LXVI.

THE RECOGNITION OF CHRIST.

" He was known of them in breaking of bread."
—LUKE xxiv. 35.

MEN have often asked whether the departed will be recognised. The risen Son of Man is recognised by that in Him which was most humble and most human. We should have thought that the token of recognition would have been selected from the least human parts of His life. We should have thought that He would have been recognised by the glory of the transfiguration mount, or by the old splendours of the miraculous power. But it is not so; that which connects His life in heaven with His life on earth is just the lowliest path that on earth He ever trod—the path of sacrifice, the hour of humiliation : " He was known of them in breaking of bread."

Wouldst thou meet and recognise thy risen Lord ? then must thou follow the disciples' way. Thou canst not, any more than they, meet Him by a flight of ecstasy, thou canst not, any more than they, find Him by a recoil from the human. It is only in the sacrifice for man that thou shalt discover the Son of Man; it is only in the breaking of the bread that Christ shall be made known to thee. Did not He tell His disciples that when He was risen from the dead, He would go before them into Galilee and invite them to meet Him there? And why into Galilee? Because Galilee was the region of the shadow of death, the place for the breaking of bread. Thee, too, He asks to meet Him in Galilee. Wouldst thou have a vision of the risen Lord? then thou must go down into the valley of His humiliation. Wouldst thou see Him as He is? then thou must be like Him in sacrificial spirit. That side of His being which heaven has not changed is just the side that is most human; He keeps the mark of the nails, He remains a high priest for ever. If thou wouldst know Him, it must be through that priesthood; if thou wouldst recognise Him, it must be through the mark of the nails borne in thine own body. If thou shalt break the bread to the hungry, if thou shalt help the fatherless and the orphan, if thou shalt lift the erring and the fallen, if thou shalt give beauty for ashes, the oil of joy for mourning, the garment of praise for the spirit of heaviness, then thou art bearing about in thy body the dying of the Lord Jesus. Thy spirit is His spirit, thy life is His life, thy love is His love, and by the power of a kindred sympathy thou knowest His love to thee; thou shalt recognise Him by that act whereby He recognises thee—the breaking of bread.

LXVII.

THE STAGES OF SPIRITUAL REST.

" *And Noah removed the covering of the ark, and looked,
and behold, the face of the ground was dry.   And in
the second month, on the seven and twentieth day of
the month, was the earth dried.   And God spake unto
Noah, saying, Go forth of the ark, thou and thy wife,
and thy sons, and thy sons' wives with thee.*"—GEN.
viii. 13–16.

THERE are three kinds of spiritual rest in this
world—the rest of outlook, the rest of experience, and the rest of action.   They are
progressive in their order.   First of all there
comes to me a time when the covering of
my ark is removed, and I am permitted to
look out upon the waters.   The flood has not
ceased, but the face of the ground is dry.   It is
as yet only a rest of outlook, a prophetic rest,
a promise of rest to come, yet even as such it
is beautiful.   Faith sees in advance of experience, and tells that Ararat is at hand.   Then
there comes to me a second rest—the rest of

experience itself; the earth itself is dried, and
my ark reposes in the very midst of the world.
It is a wondrous advance on the rest of outlook; I was then tossing even amid the vision
of hope, I am now calm in experience of dry
land. Yet one stage is wanted to make me
perfect; I am still within my ark, and therefore still separate from the world. I must be
able to rest outside of my ark, I must be able
to be calm in the midst of that very world
which once constituted my flood; my triumph
is complete when God says to my soul, "Go
forth of the ark."

O Thou who art the true Ararat, the true
rest of my spirit, perfect Thy rest in me.
Give me the outlook of faith whereby I
shall anticipate the coming glory, and see the
dayspring ere yet it is dawn. Give me the
calm of experience whereby I shall repose
within my ark, even though the voices of the
world are around me, the power to keep amid
change Thy peace that passeth understanding.
Give me yet one more boon, and that the
highest of all—the power to go forth from the
ark itself and to rest in the very work of the

L

world. My rest is not complete until it is
rest in action, my peace is not perfect until
it is Thy peace—the peace that could endure
under the shadow of a cross. Give me Thy
Divine power to sleep amid the storm, to be
calm amid the turmoil, to be restful where
the world finds unrest. Then shall I be able
to dispense with my ark of seclusion. I shall
go out to meet the flood, and its waters shall
not overwhelm me. I shall have liberty to
mingle in the scenes that once would have
been my destruction. I shall have strength
to meet the pleasures that once would have
drowned my soul. My life of faith shall be
my life of perfect freedom in that hour when
Thou shalt say to my spirit, "Go forth of the
ark."

LXVIII.

THE ROAD TO GREATNESS.

" So when they had dined, Jesus saith to Simon Peter, Simon, son of Jonas, lovest thou me more than these? He saith unto Him, Yea, Lord; Thou knowest that I love Thee. He saith unto him, Feed my lambs."— JOHN xxi. 15.

"Lovest thou me more than these love me?" It is an appeal to the oldest instinct of Peter's nature—his desire to be first. The root of his whole being had been ambition. Even in his approach to his Lord there had been a consciousness of self, a thirst for superiority, a desire that his coming should be singled out from the approaches of all other men. " Bid *me* that I come to Thee on the waters "—that had been the motto of his life. What was he that he should be bidden more than John or James or Nathaniel ? But the instinct for superiority was *in* the man, and he could not help it. And now it is to this instinct that our Lord appeals, " Lovest thou me more than these love me ?" is there the old wish to be first. But observe the new revelation which the Lord makes to the old instinct, " Feed my lambs." It is as if he said : Peter, thou hast been pursuing a wrong road to greatness ; he that is least shall be greatest of all. Wouldst thou be spiritually the most conspicuous of the band ? Then must thou be the least proud, the most self-forgetting. Thou must come down to feed the very lambs of the flock. Thou must descend into the lowliest valleys of the world. Thou must lose through the very power of thy love all sense of thine own power. Thou must forget thine interest in the interest of the lives beneath thee, thou must be oblivious of thy wants in feeling the hunger and the thirst of other souls, thou must take no thought for thyself through the pressure of the one great thought —the burden of humanity, the bearing of my cross.

O Thou that hast emptied Thyself of Thy glory, and by Thy humiliation hast conquered the world, help me to be great like Thee *in* Thee. Give me Thine own spirit of self-forgetfulness, that I may be inspired with the power of love. Teach me to lose self-will, that I may be strengthened by a higher will. Let my life be buried in the love of Thee, hid in the sense of Thy presence, absorbed and lost and overshadowed in Thine all-excelling glory. Then in Thy cross shall I reach Thy crown, and Calvary shall become my Olivet. My enthusiasm of self-forgetfulness shall be the greatness of my power, my loss shall be my gain, my death shall be the strength of my life. When I feel that I have nothing I shall indeed possess all things ; when I am least conscious of myself I shall be strongest of all. Teach me to feed Thy lambs.

LXIX.

THE DARK THINGS OF LIFE.

" He discovereth deep things out of darkness, and bringeth out to light the shadow of death."—JOB xii. 22.

THE things which give us most evidence of God are just the dark things of life; this was the experience of the man who, of all others, knew most of life's dark things. And what Job learned by his sorrow we are all learning —that the cross is our crown, that the rejected stone is the head of the corner. Thou art seeking light on the life beyond the grave— light that shall dispel the gloom of death and turn back its shadow. But it does not occur to thee that the shadow of death is itself to be the light that thou seekest. " He bringeth out to light the shadow of death," says Job, —causes illumination to come from the very source which threatened to shut it out for ever. It is from thy vision of death that there comes to thee the clearest sight thou hast of immortality. Hast thou not seen how often at the evening time there has been light? Hast thou not marked how, when the outer man was perishing, the inner was renewing day by day? Hast thou not beheld how, when flesh and heart fainted and failed, when the silver cord was being loosed and the golden bowl was nearly broken, the eye of faith grew preternaturally bright, and the heart of love preternaturally strong? And

in that preternatural brightness thou didst
learn that earth was not all, that there was
something which could still live, yea, which
could vividly live even when the old nature
had been overshadowed. It was out of the
shadow that thy hope came, it was death that
revealed the power of a higher life.

My soul, do not despise the shadows of life.
Do not say that they are exceptions to the
proof of Divine Intelligence ; do not exclaim
when they are passing over thee that thy way
is hid from the Lord.   These shadows are sent
to thee, not as hidings, but as *revelations* of
the face of God ; they come to thee as messengers of light.   They tell thee what thou
couldst not know without them—that there is
a life stronger than the natural life.   How
couldst thou learn that, if the natural life
never failed thee ?   How could faith begin
if sight were perfect ?   How could trust exist
if there were no darkness?   It is the darkness
that lights thee, it is from the shadows that
thy spiritual nature is illuminated.   From the
sense of human emptiness thou reachest that
prophetic hunger which is certain to be filled;

thy life rises, phœnix-like, from the ashes of
thy dying, and out of thy deepest darkness
God says, " Let there be light."

LXX.

THE ARM OF THE LORD.

" *Who hath believed our report? and to whom is the arm of
the Lord revealed?   For He shall grow up before Him
as a tender plant, and as a root out of a dry ground.*"
—Isa. liii. 1, 2.

THE prophet believed himself to be speaking a
paradox, a thing which no man would naturally credit.   And so he was.   Who, indeed,
would naturally believe that the arm or power
of the Lord could be revealed in that which all
men, in all times, have associated with powerlessness ?   We seek for the revelations of
God's power in the strong things of life—in
battle, lightning, and tempest, in thunder,
earthquake, and fire.   But we do not seek for
them in the endurance of life's privations—in
the struggling growth of the tender plant, or

in the root that springs from a dry ground.
These are to us the symbols of powerlessness ;
we say, the arm of the Lord is not there.
Yet, to the eye of the prophet, it is just in
these things that God shows His arm ; the
highest revelation of His might is in the gentleness of Him who grew up as a tender plant.
Is it not so to us too ?   What is to thee the
mightiest sign of God in this world ? is it
not the life of Him who had power to *lay
down* His life.   What is to thee the strongest
manifestation of will in this world ? is it not
the strength of Him who said, "Not as I
will, but as Thou wilt." What is to thee the
greatest exhibition of unweariedness in this
world ? is it not the exhaustlessness of that
love which cried, "Come unto me all ye that
labour and are heavy laden, and I will give
you rest."

O Thou Divine power which men called
weakness, reveal Thine arm to me.   Reveal to
me the omnipotent strength that was unconsciously eulogised in the words, " He saved
others ; Himself He cannot save." The world
thought it was a sign of impotence, but it

was strength unspeakable, such strength as belonged only to Thee. That inability of Thine was the greatest force in this universe— the power of love. It was the power of Thy love that made Thee powerless to save Thyself, that would not let Thee turn aside from the narrow road and the dolorous way, that impelled Thee to tread the garden and to climb the cross. O strong Son of God, whose strength was to say, " I cannot save myself," be that strength also mine ; reveal Thine arm *in* me, as well as *to* me. Make me strong to bear the cross, to despise the shame, to endure contradiction against myself, to prefer the narrow path of duty to the kingdoms of the world and their glory. Make me strong to trample self under my feet, to surrender my will to Thy will, to yield up my spirit to the crucifying hand of love; then shall I know what that saying meaneth, " The power of God unto salvation."

LXXI.

SPIRITUAL ADMIRATION.

" When we shall see Him, there is no beauty that we
should desire Him."—Isa. liii. 2.

THE boundary between spiritual death and
spiritual life is admiration. Between seeing
the beauty without desiring it and seeing the
beauty *with* desire there seems but a thin line,
but it is the line of infinitude ; it is the difference between the almost and the altogether.
Admiration of Christ's beauty is the lowest
step of the ladder, but it *is* a step. It may
exist where the deeds of life are not yet in
harmony with its ideal, but it is the prophecy
of the future perfection, the pledge of good
things to come. My soul, bethink thee, that
which thou admirest must be allied to thyself.
Thou couldst not possibly admire if it had
nothing in common with thee. Like can only
be known by like ; love cannot be recognised
by selfishness, nor can the face of purity be
beheld by moral debasement. Therefore it is

that the words are written, "Without holiness no man shall see the Lord." It is not
a threat ; it is the statement of a divine law
which is also a human law. Thou canst not
see anything which is not already in thee.
Thou canst not see beauty if thou hast not the
sense of beauty, thou canst not hear music if
thou hast not the thrill of harmony, thou canst
not love virtue if thou hast not the germ of
goodness. If, when Jesus of Nazareth passeth
by, thou hast felt a glow of admiration, a
longing to be like Him and a thirsting to
be near Him—by that admiring glow thou
knowest that already He has been with thee.
Thou couldst not kindle at His presence if
His presence were alien to thine, thou couldst
not imitate His likeness if conformity to His
image had not even now begun. All imitation
is the fruit of some likeness ; it does not
precede but follow the conformity of nature.
That to which thou aspirest is the shadow of
something already hidden in thy heart, and it
is this that makes thine aspiration precious.
In the longing of thy heart for Him the Son
of Man beholds Himself in thee ; in the

approach of thy spirit to Him He learns that His Spirit has drawn near to thee. The beauty by which thou seest Him is His own beauty, the love with which thou longest for Him is His own love, the light by which thou seekest Him is His own light. Thy longing is the measure of thee, thy conscious want is the test of thy possibilities, thine aspiration is the prophecy of thy stature; the beauty of the Lord is in thee when thou hast seen and desired His beauty.

LXXII.

THE PROVIDENCE OF SORROW.

" He knoweth thy walking through this great wilderness."
—DEUT. ii. 7.

Is there, then, a Providence so individual as that? Is there a Divine knowledge extending even to the greatness of my solitude, to the uttermost loneliness of that walk through which I seemed to travel in the valley of death's shadow. That was of all others the time when I thought myself to be walking alone. The wilderness was very vast and very dreary, and in the midst of its vastness and its dreariness my life appeared to me but as a vapour and vanity. My God seemed to have passed by on the other side, and I cried out from dawn to evening that my way was hid from Him. And yet at that very time it was all known—my wilderness and its vastness and its dreariness. When I thought that my way was hid in the obscurity of a desert, the very steps of my walk through that desert were being marked and numbered. Wherefore should I have ever doubted it? Looking back from the conquered land of promise I can see that the wilderness was no accident, no separation from the plan of God. I can see that the hour when I seemed to be most distant from the Father's eye was just the hour in which He was in closest contact with my soul. My wilderness was my garden; there, unknown to me but not unknown to Him, the seeds were being sown that, in the land of promise, were to become trees of righteousness. There, in what appeared to me the silence and the solitude, the chords of my heart were being strung for richest music, and the pulses of my heart were being quickened for social life—the life of the city of God. It was to me what it was made to my Lord—the middle way between two glories. It separated the glory of my past from the glory of my future. Behind me lay the waters of Jordan, where I saw the opened heavens; before me lay the glorified feast of Cana, where the water of life was to be made wine. And the desert was between; the old was left behind, and the new had not yet come. Yet the desert was better than the old, and it was leading to the new. It had shut me out from the romance of Jordan that it might teach me how real and earnest was life's struggle, and in the very reality and earnestness it was preparing me for the city of God. Therefore my walk through the wilderness was a walk with Him. He was leading me all the time by green pastures and quiet waters; the Lord was in that place and I knew it not. Where shall I build my monument of deepest gratitude? Not amid the

flowers shall I raise it, not amid the days
when the glitter of life was around me, not
even amid the hours when the first fervour of
a new life burst upon me, but amid the silence
and the solitude and the struggle of that
wilderness journey, where, for the first time,
I felt my nothingness, because, for the first
time, I had felt the power of God.

LXXIII.

THE SONG OF SACRIFICE.

" *Sacrifice and offering Thou didst not desire; mine ears
hast Thou opened. . . . Then said I, Lo, I come.
. . . I delight to do Thy will, O my God.*"—Ps. xl.
6–8.

"Mine ears hast Thou opened." It is as if the
Psalmist had caught the sound of a far-off
strain of music, a music of preternatural loveliness. It is as if he said, I hear what I never
heard before—a song in whose tones there is
not a chord of sadness, in whose melody there
is not a note of gloom, but only praise—

unqualified, incessant praise. And what was the burden of this new song to which the Psalmist listened with open ears? It was the voice of One as yet far distant, but who was drawing ever nearer with a new message to the soul. And the message which He was foreshadowing was this: Ye men of Israel, I tell you that there is a time coming when there shall be no more pain. Your religion is now all pain together; you are serving God with sacrifice, with fear, with trembling. There is no joy in your approach to the Infinite Glory; your very gifts are wrung from you, and you value what you give by your difficulty in giving it. But I am coming to reveal to you a more excellent way—not to abolish the gift, but to abolish the sacrifice. I am coming to give to your Father in heaven a donation that in all the years He has never received before—the delight of a human heart. I am coming to yield up to His service a tribute which was never before thought to be in a servant's power to give—the offering of a free will, the surrender of a voluntary life. I will not offer my pain but my joy. You have

M

yielded up to your Father only the cries of tortured victims; I shall yield up in your behalf a life whose constant dying shall be its constant song of praise. " Lo, I come: I delight to do Thy will, O my God."

Son of Man, Thou who hast ushered in this day of painless worship, help me to enter into Thy joy. Breathe on me that I may receive the same Divine Spirit—the spirit of surrender without sense of sacrifice. Teach me day by day that what my Father wishes is not my Gethsemane, but my will; not my experience of suffering, but my power to rejoice in Him in *spite* of my experience of suffering. Reveal to me that my sacrifice is never perfect in my Father's sight until in the view of my spirit it is a sacrifice no more. Then and only then shall I know what it is to be made comformable unto Thy death, to have fellowship with Thy suffering, to be in communion with Thy cross. I shall learn that dying is life, that loss is gain, that perfect sacrifice is fulness of joy. There shall be no more death, there shall be no more pain, there shall be no more tears, for the former things shall have passed

away, when through Thy Spirit I shall be
able to say, "I delight to do Thy will, O
my God."

———

LXXIV.

CHRISTIAN FREEDOM.

" The perfect law of liberty."—JAS. i. 25.

LAW and liberty. To the natural mind these
are the greatest contrasts in the world. To
the heart of youth liberty presents itself as the
breaking of law. The tempter comes to the
young man and says, Why are you not free? it
is an unmanly thing to be constantly under
restraint; come, break your fetters, and be
master of yourself. That is the voice of sin to
every opening life, and it is a plausible voice;
it promises a thing which we all value and
which we all ought to value—freedom. It
offers to give us that very boon which Christ
expressly came to give—liberty. But now
observe the difference between the mode of the
tempter and the mode of the Divine Master.

The tempter says, You will be free by *breaking* the law ; Christ says, You will be free by *perfecting* the law. Ponder these words of the Apostle, "The perfect law of liberty." He says, So far is restraint from being the enemy of freedom, it is the *want* of restraint that prevents perfect freedom ; if law were perfect, if it were only sufficiently binding, if it could only obtain an undivided mastery over your soul, you would instantaneously be free—free as the winds of heaven, free as the child at play.

My soul, dost thou marvel at this doctrine ? Dost thou not know that perfect law is love, and that where the spirit of love is there is liberty ? Before love comes, the law is not perfectly thy master ; it is only without thee. But when love comes. the law has possessed thee altogether ; it has taken thy citadel,— the heart. And this possession is thy perfect freedom. Thou art never free in any pursuit until the love of that pursuit has mastered thee. Then, for the first time, thy will breaks forth into spontaneous action, and thy heart rejoices in the voluntary choice of its labour.

Thy most glorious moment, the moment in which the charter of thy freedom is for ever signed, is in the hour when thou art compelled to say, " I cannot help it," the hour when love has become such a necessity of thy heart, such a law of thy life, that thou hast no longer any choice but to obey. The compulsion of thy heart is thy perfect freedom ; when love shall take thee prisoner, captivity itself shall be taken captive. O golden chain, O glorious servitude, O free necessity, be thine my freedom evermore. Take possession of my heart, my reason, my understanding, my will. Enthrone Thyself in the empire of my being, that, in Thy sense of mastery, I may learn for the first time what it is to be free, and know what it is to be at rest. When I shall take Thy yoke upon me, I shall find rest unto my soul, for the yoke of Thy love is perfect joy, and the law of Thy life is perfect liberty.

LXXV.

THE PRESERVATION OF PERSONALITY IN THE CHRISTIAN LIFE.

" That God may be all in all."—1 COR. xv. 28.

AM I, then, to be lost in God? Is my whole personal life to be absorbed and overshadowed in the life of the Infinite One? Am I to have no more separate being than one of those myriad drops which compose the vast ocean? If so, then my goal is death indeed. If my personality is to melt into the being of God as a cloud melts into the blaze of sunshine, then, surely, is God not my life but my annihilation. He can no longer say of me, " Because *I* live, thou shalt live also." Nay, but, my soul, thou hast misread the destiny of thy being. It is not merely written that God is to be all, but that He is to be all *in* all. *His* universal life is not to destroy the old varieties of being ; it is to pulsate through these varieties. His music is to fill the world, but it is to sound through all the varied instruments of the world. His sunshine is to flood the universe, but it is to be mirrored in a thousand various forms. His love is to penetrate creation, but it is to be reflected in the infinite diversities of the hearts and souls of men. Thou speakest of losing thyself in the ocean of His love, but this is only poetically true. Love is an ocean where no man permanently loses himself; he regains himself in richer, nobler form. The only ocean in which a man loses himself is self-love; God's love gives him back his life that he may keep it unto life eternal. Thou art not thyself until thou hast found God. Wouldst thou truly behold thyself? then must thou with open face behold as in a glass His glory. Thou wilt never become a power to thyself until God has become all in thee; thou wilt never really live until thou hast lived in Him. Forget thyself, my soul. Forget thy pride and thy selfishness, thy cares and thy crosses, thy world which thou bearest within thee. Unbar the doors of thy being to the sunshine of that other Presence that already stands without, waiting to get in. And, verily, thy forgetfulness shall make thee strong, thy surrender shall make thee mighty, thy dying unto self shall make thee alive for evermore. Thy form shall be beautiful when it is gilded by His light, thy voice shall be melodious when it is tuned by His music, thy heart shall be on fire when it is quickened by His love; thou shalt be everything when God shall be all.

LXXVI.

ADAPTATION.

" He hath made everything beautiful in His time."
—ECCLES. iii. 11.

WHAT! everything? sorrow and trial, and privation and weariness, and struggle? Surely these are not the things which one would call beautiful, and surely much of life has been made up of these? Yes, but, my soul, God has made even these things for thee, and He has made them to contribute to thy beauty. There is a time in which sorrow is beautiful as there is a time in which childhood is beautiful; as there is a time in which winter is beautiful. It is the time that justifies the sorrow; its beauty lies in its seasonableness. Is it not written that when the fulness of time was come God sent His Son—sent into this world the greatest manifestation of a cross which the world has ever seen? It was the fulness of the time that justified the fulness of the sorrow, that made the fulness of the sorrow beautiful. The world had reached that stage of hardness which needed to be crucified, and therefore the crucifixion came. It came not a day too soon, nor a day too late; it was the act suited to the hour, it was beautiful in its time. So, my soul, has it ever been, shall it ever be, with thee. God never sends His cross into thy heart until thy heart is absolutely ripe for it, until it is the only fruit that would fit thy year. Thou speakest of the adaptations of nature, and verily all adaptation is beautiful. Thou sayest that the eye was made for sunshine, that the ear was made for melody, that the heart was made for joy. Yea, but there are times in which the eye was made for darkness, there are times in which the ear was made for discord, there are times in which the heart was made for sorrow. If thou knewest the *time* of thy visitation it would be to thee the best and costliest of all thy Father's gifts. Thinkest thou that the wilderness is an accident? It is that which prevents accident, which keeps thee from becoming a spontaneous flower of the field. It is that which forces thee to hold thy virtue as a conscious possession. It sends clouds into thine understanding that thine understanding may become faith. It sends temptation into thine innocence that thine innocence may become purity. It sends bereavement into thy heart that thy heart may become awake to its infinite power of loving. If thou wert a plant the calm would to thee alone be beautiful, but because thou art a man thou hast need also of the storm. One day thou shalt bless God for the cloud as well as for the sunshine; He has made them both beautiful, each in its time.

LXXVII.

THE BUILDING OF THE SOUL.

" And the house when it was in building, was built of stone made ready before it was brought thither : so that there was neither hammer nor axe nor any tool of iron heard in the house while it was in building."—1 KINGS vi. 7.

ONE would think, from such words as these, that there was no room for struggle in the religious life, nor in the conversion into that life. The whole building grows up softly, silently, almost mystically, and we are tempted to feel as if there were no sympathy in that temple with the wrestling of our hearts. Nay, but hast thou forgotten that the struggle was all past ere ever the building was begun? Hast thou forgotten that the stone was "made ready before it was brought thither?" What a world of meaning lies unspoken in that little clause? Before these stones came into unity they all existed in individual separation, in isolation, in solitude. Before they passed

into the stage of silent building they had each to go through a process of noise and conflict, had each to be hewn into symmetry with its place in the coming temple. There is a great unrecorded battle of the spiritual life hinted at in this *making ready*; it is but a flash of thought, but it is a flash that lights up our whole experience and reveals us to ourselves. It tells us that the silence is not the first but the last thing, that there is a making ready for the symmetry ere the symmetry is reached. It tells us that Saul of Tarsus has his struggle ere the light from heaven breaks upon his view—that conflict where he finds it so hard to kick against the goads. It tells us that Nicodemus has his solitary walk by night ere he can take up the dead Christ from the shadow of the cross — that solitary walk wherein he feels deserted by the old and not yet convinced by the new. And marvellously comforting is this message which it brings to many a struggling soul. Art thou perplexed by thine inward disquietude? Art thou tossed upon a sea of doubt and wrapt in a mist of uncertainty? Art thou experiencing

Perplexed

the accusations of a conscience that speaks louder and louder every day ? Say not that, therefore, there is no place for thee within the silence of the mystic temple ; it is just therefore that there *is* a place for thee. This struggle of thine is thy making ready. This loudness of thy conscience is the hewing of thy hardness into symmetry—the symmetry that will fit thee to be a stone in the temple of Christ. Thy solitude is not the neglect of thee, thy struggle is not the absence of thy God from thee ; it is the eye of thy God *upon* thee. He has taken thee up to the wilderness that He may make thee ready. All the pain He sends thee is the sign of His interest in thee, the proof that He is preparing thee for the symmetry of the temple of peace. Thy wilderness is the vestibule into thy heaven. Bless the Lord, O my soul.

LXXVIII.

THE HELP OF GOD.

" He was marvellously helped till he was strong."
—2 CHRON. xxvi. 15.

THERE are two kinds of help in this world;
there is marvellous help, and there is natural
help. The marvellous help declines as the power
of natural help grows. There is a time when
we cannot help ourselves, and then everything
is provided for us; we are guided by instinct
as the bee is guided. Infancy is the most
helpless of all periods so far as our self-help
goes, yet perhaps it is the period of our least
danger. We have then God's marvellous help
—the provision of maternal love and our own
childlike instinct of obedience. We are led
by a thousand influences, not one of which we
have foreseen, not one of which we recognise
even when it appears. But as our natural
strength grows, God's supernatural strength
is gradually withdrawn, and when we have

reached the promised land of our human nature the miraculous manna ceases. Say not that, therefore, God has *Himself* withdrawn ; remember that what thou callest nature is God's help also. When thou wert young and nature was weak He helped thee marvellously, supernaturally ; when thou art full-grown and nature is strong He helps thee naturally—co-operates with thy nature, becomes a fellow-worker with thee. Dost thou see more of the supernatural in the lower than in the human creation ? Say not on that account that there is less provision made for man. It is just the provision made for man that has caused the manna to cease. Knowest thou how dear to the heart of God it is to have a fellow-worker with Himself—one that feels what He feels, and whose spirit is helping with His own ? Knowest thou how dear it is even to the earthly father when he learns for the first time that his being is no longer supernatural to the heart of his child, when, for the first time, the heart of his child works with *his* heart, helps with his help, strives with his aim, feels with his desire ? That is an earthly father's joy because in that hour he knows that he is not supernatural to his child any more, but that their natures are for ever one. So is it with thy heavenly Father when He sees His Christ in thee; He reaches then the true parental joy. 'Tis then He knows that the partition wall is broken between Him and thee, that heaven and earth have met together. 'Tis then He knows that He no longer stands over thee as a lawgiver, or dictates to thee as a sovereign, for He beholds thee strong with His strength, natural with His nature, able to work with Him, because His spirit has become thine own. Happy art thou, my soul, when thy strength shall be so perfected to thy Father's eye that He shall send thee no more the help that is marvellous, but shall ask thee to work with Him in that human helpfulness which is the life of Christ.

LXXIX.

DIVINE EDUCATION.

" I taught Ephraim also to go, taking them by their arms ;
but they knew not that I healed them."—HOSEA xi. 3.

THOU sayest that this world is a scene of proba-
tion ; no, it is not, it is a place of education.
God has placed thee here not to prove thee but
to teach thee—to hold thee by the arms until
thou shalt learn to walk. What need to put
thee into the world to prove that by nature
thou canst not walk ? What need to bring
thee into life only that thou mayest sit for
thy portrait and reveal thy blemishes in the
light of eternity ? If this were all the design
of thy being it were indeed a waste of being.
Thy Father hath made thee for something
other than that—not to prove thine impotence
but to train thy footsteps, not to reveal thy
blemishes but to perfect thy beauty. Thy
God is educating thee. Very beautiful is the
metaphor by which He describes His educa-

N

tion of the world : it is **that of a** mother train-
ing the steps of her child. She stands at a
seeming distance and says, "Come." She
stands at a seeming distance, but all **the time**
the intervening space is bridged by the arms
of love. There is not a moment's break in the
continuity of that grasp with which she holds
her treasure. She seeks but to awaken within her child that pride of new responsibility
which comes from the semblance of being
alone, to make it feel as if it *were* independent
by the exercise of its own power. Nor does
she tell it that she is teaching it to walk. We
are best taught when we are taught unconsciously. She tempts it towards her with some
glittering prize, some bright bauble, some
sparkling reward, and the little feet know not
that the true prize is their own healing, the
true reward their own power of exercise. So,
too, is it with thy heavenly Father. He
tempts thee on thy way, on *His* way, by
something which is not His object, nor which
yet is thy goal. He shows thee a glittering
bauble at the end of the way, and says,
"Come ; " He tempts thee by a promised land

into a land that transcends the promise. Thou knowest not that He heals thee. It seems to thee that thou art being led by the green pastures only that thou mayest gather the flowers of earthly pleasure. Yet all the time thou art being conducted by a way that thou knowest not into a city of habitation of which thou dost not dream. Thy Father's end for thee is better than thine own end for thyself; thine is only the earthly Canaan, His is the heavenly Christ. The promised land thou art seeking is at best but poor and fleeting, but in thy march towards it thou art gaining what thou dost not seek—the lesson of a walk with God.

LXXX.

THE SECRET OF THE LORD.

"A new name written, which no man knoweth saving he that receiveth it."—REV. ii. 17.

THERE is a secret word which admits men into the Christian society, but it is a word that is spoken only to the heart; it is the word *peace.* This is the secret of the Lord that is with them that fear Him. The peace of Christ in the soul to the eye of an outward beholder is indeed a secret. He cannot explain it, he cannot account for it, he cannot understand it; it seems to him as if it had no right to be. He sees men joyous where he would be miserable, restful where he would be perplexed, calm where he would be appalled, and he asks, Whence is it so? There is a peace which does not pass understanding, which the world understands quite well, and can refer to reasonable causes. Wealth, fame, rank, power, freedom from the tossings and the heavings of the great sea of human trouble, anchorage within some earthly haven on which the storms never blow—all this the world can appreciate as a source of peace. But where riches are not, where fame and power are not, where freedom from the storm is not found, where the haven of anchorage is not known,—there the world wonders to find unbroken joy. It marvels to see rest amid unrest, calm amid storm, light amid darkness, love amid shadow, life amid death; the peace of Christ is to it a secret.

My soul, it must be a secret to thee too even after thou hast possessed it. Thou hearest the sound of the wind, but canst not tell whence it cometh; so is it with the peace of Christ within thee. When that peace is within thee thou hast, indeed, a joy, but it is a joy thyself dost not understand; it passeth even thy knowledge. It lies beneath all human causes, it is independent of all human circumstances. Thou canst no more tell why thy heart shines than thou canst tell why the sun shines; it shines because it has become its nature so to do. It gets not its light from aught without, nay, it shall give its light to everything without—even to the shadows. It is not kindled by the glow of worldly fortune, nay, it will impart its own glow even to worldly *misfortune*, will turn everything it touches into gold. O Divine Peace, that art a contradiction to them that know Thee not and a secret even to them that know Thee, let me be a sharer in Thy power. Let me experience the marvel of Thy presence within me without

seeking to solve the marvel. Let me be content to be a secret unto myself, a wonder
to the law of my own being. Let me know
what it is to have the incomprehensible joy,
the unexplainable rest, the stillness that cannot be stirred though the earth be removed
and the mountains be cast into the depths of
the sea. Let me experience the Divine sleep
in the midst of the waves—the sleep that Thou
promisest to Thy beloved; so shall I learn
what it is to possess the secret of the Lord.

———

LXXXI.

IN THE HANDS OF GOD.

*" It is a fearful thing to fall into the hands of the living
God."*—HEB. x. 31.

YEA, but it is a more fearful thing still *not* to
fall into His hands. To fall into His hands
must be pain, for the passage from death into
life is ever painful. The first sensation of an
infant is pain, just because life has come and
is in struggle with the old elements of death.

There is a fear in all life which does not exist in lifelessness, for the sense of life is in its nature an awful thing. But wouldst thou, therefore, rather be without it? wouldst thou, therefore, rather be a clod of the valley? Nay, for the very awfulness of the possession is itself thy glory. So is it with thy spiritual life. When it comes to thee it comes with a great sense of pain. It wakens thee up to the fearfulness, to the awfulness, of being a responsible soul. It tells thee that thou art in the presence of a law which thou hast violated, that thou art in the midst of an universe with which thou art not in unison. It quickens thee into the knowledge that there is impurity within thyself, and causes thee to cry out, "O wretched man that I am!" It is only when the pure life comes that the impure life is revealed. It is only when the pure life comes that the impure life begins to struggle. The struggle of thy soul is the fruit of thy new birth. The old life was a stagnant pool; the new is a waving sea. Its waves are its glory, its storms are the signs of its higher destiny.

O God, Thou living God, let me fall into Thy hands; it is only in Thy hands that I can be perfectly safe. I know that to fall into Thy hands is indeed a fearful thing; I know that it is the beginning of all my fears, for it is the beginning of all my responsibilities. In Thy hands I shall learn the awfulness of my spiritual being, in Thy hands I shall learn how little it has fulfilled its destiny. Nevertheless, it is in Thy hands alone that I would be; the fear that comes from contact with Thee is indeed the beginning of wisdom. There would be no penalty to me so great as to fall *out* of Thy hands; to be out of Thy hands is to be dead. There is a pain *with* Thee, which is not found without Thee, but it is the pain of love which is the pain of the life Divine. Translate me into that life. Lift me into union with Thine own Divine being. Raise me into fellowship with that power of Thy love which is the power of Thy suffering. Take me into Thy hands and hold me in Thy fear. Let me learn in Thy life how solemn is my own, let me see in Thy glory how poor is my own. I will not shrink from the fear of beholding in a glass the image of my moral deformity, if only I know that the glass wherein I behold it has been fashioned by the hands of the living God.

LXXXII.

THE REVEALING PAST.

" Hitherto hath the Lord helped us."—1 SAM. vii. 12.

MY Father, I am ever seeking from Thee a new revelation, and I am ever saying that Thou art silent. Yet it is only my own heart that is silent. I am seeking Thy revelation in the wrong direction; I am asking it from my future, and lo, it is coming from my past. The vision of my past is not a vision of old things; they are all renewed in the light of retrospect. The newest of all revelations is the life of my past when seen in Thee; it is like the difference between passing through a landscape at night and looking down upon the same landscape from the brow of the hill at

morning. My past is so transfigured in retrospect that I would not have known it. Spots
that looked barren when I was passing through,
appear in looking back as scenes of luxuriant
verdure. Events that seemed adverse in the
watches of the night are transformed by the
morning beam into messages of blessing.
Crosses that pressed upon my soul in wander-
ing through the wilderness are seen from the
promised land to have been exceeding weights
of glory, and it is almost with a cry of surprise
that I exclaim, " Hitherto hath the Lord helped
me." The marvel of Thy revelation is its
glorification of my rejected circumstances; the
stones which the builder refused have been
made the head of the corner. I have got more
from Thee than faith promised. Faith only promised that Thou wouldst help me *in spite* of
these circumstances, but lo, Thou hast made
these circumstances themselves my helpers.
Faith only promised that Thou wouldst
deliver my soul from its struggles, but lo,
Thou hast revealed to me that my struggles
were themselves the agents of Thy deliverance.
Faith only promised that notwithstanding the

wilderness I would be brought safely to the land of rest, but lo, Thou hast shown me that the wilderness was itself the very portal to that land. Therefore, my past is to me a new revelation of Thyself. Thou hast not suffered me to see the *hereafter*, but Thou hast allowed me to behold the *hitherto*, and verily the hitherto is glorious. No vision of the future glory could to me be more wondrous, more divine, than is this sight of the glory of my past. I see it from the Mount of Transfiguration, and it is all new ; its face is shining, its garments are glistening. I will raise a monument to the glory of my past ; I will build it with the rejected stones that I left despised by the wayside, and I will write upon it the record of Thy guiding love, " Hitherto hath the Lord helped us."

LXXXIII.

THE ANSWER TO CHRIST'S PRAYER.

" *Who in the days of His flesh, when He had offered up prayers and supplications, with strong crying and tears, unto Him that was able to save Him from death, and was heard in that He feared.*"— HEB. V. 7.

"WAS heard in that He feared;" was it so? I had always thought that His was an un- answered prayer. Did the bitter cup pass from His lips when, in the solitude of the Gethsemane shadows, He cried unto His Father? did there come to Him that respite from death which seemed to be the object of His prayer? Nay, for that was not the object of His prayer; that desire was only expressed conditionally, "if it be *possible,* let this cup pass from me." But there was a desire in the depths of His heart which was expressed unconditionally; it was the prayer that His human will might be one with the Divine will. "He was heard in that He *feared,"* says the sacred writer; His fear was the beautiful thing which caused His prayer to be accepted. Fear is not generally beautiful, it is not commonly a virtue at all. What was there about this fear of Jesus which made. it so precious in the Father's sight? It was this—His was not the fear of death, but the dread of human frailty. He was afraid lest the weakness of the flesh should make Him choose a path different from the path His Father had chosen for Him. He was afraid lest even in desire He should follow a road less dolorous than that which His Father had prepared, and the strong crying of His spirit came forth in the earnest supplication, "Not as I will, but as Thou wilt." That was the prayer which His Father answered, and in the answer to that prayer the cause of His fear vanished. The answer came not in the rolling back of death but in the strengthening of His spirit for death, not in the passing of the cup, but in the passing of the bitterness from the cup; the garden of Gethsemane was conquered when the angels appeared to strengthen Him.

Son of Man, let me be a sharer in Thy
Divine strength. I, too, have my Gethsemanes,
where there are shadows without and fears
within and solitudes around. At these times
my soul is troubled, and I know not what I
shall ask. The dark hour which has come to
me may have been the hour for which I was
made, and I dare not say unconditionally,
"Father, save me from this hour." But in
Thy strength, O Son of Man, I shall have all
I need and more. If the Spirit that fortified
Thee shall become my spirit, I shall be strong
with Thy Divine strength. Unite my will to
Thy will, that Thy experience may become
mine own. Help me to *learn of Thee*, that
the yoke of life may be eased without being
diminished, that the burden of life may be
lightened without being lessened. Help me to
experience that new power of the eye which
shall make it unnecessary to roll away the
clouds of night, that new strength of the arm
which shall cause it to be unneeded that the
outward weight should be removed. Let me
learn of Thee that there is an answer to prayer
which eye sees not, which ear hears not, which

history records not, which is received and recorded only in the silent depths of the soul.

––––––––––

LXXXIV.

FAITH AND KNOWLEDGE.

" And we believe and are sure that Thou art that Christ, the Son of the living God."—JOHN vi. 69.

" WE believe and are sure ; " more strictly it should be rendered, " We *have* believed and are sure." The thought of the apostle is that there has been a development in his experience ; he began by simple faith, and he has ended with assured knowledge. Such is ever the order of the Christian understanding ; we first believe, and then we know. Faith is not the opposite of knowledge ; it is the anticipation, the prophecy of knowledge. Faith is to knowledge what the swallow is to the summer—the messenger that sings its coming. Faith soars up to heaven in the morning and

sees in advance the plan of the unfolding day.
It cannot yet trace the plan, it cannot yet tell
how the plan is to *be* unfolded, but it beholds
what it cannot analyse, it trusts what it cannot verify. So was it with the Master when
He first said to His disciples, " Follow me."
Why should He have hoped that they would
follow Him ? they did not yet know Him.
But He felt that they must follow Him before
they knew Him, that they could only come to
know Him through the experience of being
near Him. And so He called upon another
faculty than knowledge; He appealed to the
power of their faith. He said, Give me the
prophetic trust of your souls. I am come to
lead you by the green pastures and beside the
quiet waters, to let you know by the walk of
experience that the pastures of life *are* green,
and that the waters of life *are* quiet. But you
can only come to know it by *walking* with me.
You must come to me without knowledge,
without proof, without experience ; you must
give me your faith. Pay me with your love *in
advance.* I do not ask it without return; I
will repay its value tenfold—in work, in sacri-

fice, but I cannot work *for* you unless you will first let me work *through* you. Grant me your sympathy beforehand. Grant me the mesmeric look of faith, that I may fill your life with my presence. Grant me the steadfast gaze of the eye, that I may transform you into my own image. Grant me the complete surrender of the will, that I may make your will my will. When I have made your will my will there shall be no more room for faith; faith shall be lost in sight, and ye shall know as ye are known. Trust me but one hour with the treasure of your hearts, and with rich interest I will give them back to you again ; lend them to me with faith, and I will restore them to you with knowledge—that knowledge of me which is life eternal. In that hour you shall be able to say, " Once we believed, now we are sure."

LXXXV.

A PROVIDENTIAL ABSENCE OF GOD.

" Lazarus is dead, and I am glad for your sakes that I was not there."—JOHN xi. 14, 15.

THERE may be a benevolent absence of God; say rather there may be an absence of God which is a phase of His providential presence. Strange at first glance read the Divine words, " I was glad that I was not there." Glad for what? Does He mean that had He been there Lazarus would not have died ? Yes, that is undoubtedly His meaning : He says just what Martha said. He felt that had He been there His human sympathy would have overcome Him, and the stroke of death would have been averted. But why be glad for this ? Martha was not glad of it, it was the special cause of her sorrow. Yes, but Martha did not see the end; she beheld only the *closing* of the grave over her dead, not its re-opening to give her dead back again. *He* beheld what Martha

did not behold. He saw the possibility of a
greater glory *through* the suffering than could
be reached without the suffering. He saw
that the shining after rain would be clearer
than the light that had never been dimmed
with tears, and He rejoiced in that momentary
absence of His person which had given to
His love so much more power to bestow.

My soul, there are times when thou lament-
est the absence of any visible sign that thy
God is near. There are seasons when thou
criest in the night, "Why art Thou so far
from helping me ? " " My way is hid from the
Lord, and my judgment is passed over from
my God." Thinkest thou that the hiding of
His face from thee comes from His forgetfulness of thee ? Nay, but from His very excess
of mindfulness. His seeming absence is itself
a form of His presence, His refusal to inter-
vene in thy sorrow is itself an act of divinest
intervention. Thy sorrow is His messenger to
thy heart, and it is a messenger of love. It
comes to bring thee a greater glory than it
takes away. It is sent to press the flower of
life to make it pour forth its perfume. It

comes to break the alabaster box, but only that
the fragrance which it imprisons within itself
may be diffused far and wide and fill the house
of humanity. Thy Father rejoices that He is
not there. He would not interfere with that
which is the discipline, the unfolding of thy
heart. He would grieve to grant thee a temporary cessation of pain at the expense of
a permanent loss of power. His best gift
to thee has been the absence of His intervening power. His best answer to thee has been
His refusal to interfere with the discipline of
thy human sorrow. His best love to thee has
been His silence in the night, when thou
madest thy petition that the night might be
removed. One day thou shalt thank Him for
His silence, one day thou shalt bless Him for
His passiveness, one day thou shalt find the
treasures of the night, and praise Thy Father
that He let thee sojourn there.

LXXXVI.

SELF-COMMUNION.

" Stand in awe, and sin not : commune with your own heart upon your bed, and be still. Offer the sacrifices of righteousness, and put your trust in the Lord."—Ps. iv. 4, 5.

THERE are four phases in the birth of the religious life—self-awakening, self-reflection, self-help, and self-abandonment. There is first the awakening of self-life to the presence of another law, a moral law which says, " Stand in awe, and sin not." There is secondly the communing of the soul with itself, the asking of that momentous question, "Am I in harmony with this moral law?" There is thirdly the effort to reach that harmony by deeds that shall create the consciousness of merit—the offering of the sacrifices of righteousness. Lastly there is the perception that the consciousness of merit is itself a want of harmony with law, and the soul by an act of self-forgetfulness loses alike its sense of merit and demerit in the trust of the living God.

My soul, wouldst thou reach this blessed conclusion? Wouldst thou arrive at this final haven of moral peace where thy weakness shall itself become thy strength? Thou mayest arrive at it, but it must be after a storm—a storm whose peculiarity shall be its inaudibleness to any ear but thine. Ere thou canst reach the final rest thou must enter into communion with thyself, must examine thine old nature in the stillness of solitude. Thine must be a struggle with thine own thoughts—a struggle where there is no clang of arms, but whose soreness lies in its very silence. How still is that communion which thy God requires of thee! "Commune with thine own heart;" what converse so silent as that? "Thine *own* heart;" not the heart of another. The heart of another would give more companionship, but it would give less test of truth. Thou mightest compare thy righteousness with the righteousness of thy brother, and go down to thy house rejoicing, and yet all the time thou mightest be in discord with the moral law of God. Only in thine own heart canst thou see thyself truly reflected, therefore it is with thyself that thy Father bids thee commune. " Commune upon thy bed ;" not alone with thine own heart, but with thine own heart in the stillest locality— in the silence of the midnight hour, where there is no distraction, and where there is no deception. There thou shalt learn what it is to be an individual soul. In the world thou art taught to forget this; thy little life is swallowed up in the crowd, and thy moral good or ill seems an indifferent thing. But here the world's judgment is reversed. When thou art alone with God the crowd melts away, and thou art to thyself an universe. Thy very sense of sin reveals to thee the infinitude of thy being. Thy very moral struggle tells thee that in spite of thyself thou art an immortal. Commune with thine own heart, O my soul.

LXXXVII.

SPIRITUAL GROWTH.

" *He brought me up also out of an horrible pit, out of the miry clay, and set my feet upon a rock, and established my goings. And He hath put a new song in my mouth, even praise unto our God: many shall see it, and fear, and shall trust in the Lord.*"—Ps. xl. 2, 3.

THE Psalmist is tracing the stages of his own experience, the successive steps by which he climbed the mount of God. At first it was only the deliverance from a dark past : " He brought me up out of an horrible pit, out of the miry clay." It was a stage of moral elevation rather than of moral fixedness, a lifting into the air, but not yet the settling on a rock. That stage came secondly. There came a time when God set his feet on a rock and established his goings. He was transported from the air to the ground, from the flight to the walk, from the mere sense of liberation to the principle of that truth which made him free. But he was not yet complete ; principle is mere duty, it is not yet love. The mind may be settled on a rock and yet the heart may be cold. He wanted not only a path for his feet but a new song for his mouth, and that which he wanted came. To the rigidness of the rock was added the heart of joy: "He hath put a new song in my mouth, even praise unto our God." One other step remained to crown, to culminate the life; the Psalmist must relinquish the thought of himself, even the thought of his own progress. He must come to value his spiritual joy, not so much for what it is as for what it can do. He must come to see that the glory of *his* salvation is its power to be the salvation of others; his life will be complete when he shall say, "Many shall see it, and fear, and shall trust in the Lord."

My soul, that progress must be thine also. Marvel not that thou art not instantaneously in possession of the fulness of joy; there is much to be done within thee ere the new song shall come. Thine must at first be only the sense of deliverance, of emancipation from the pit and from the mire. The weaning from the old does not at once bring the joy of the new. Thou mayest come even to rest on the settled rock without an immediate entrance into that joy; the power of duty may make thee strong without yet making thee buoyant. But the hour of love is at hand, and will not tarry—the hour when the walk of the feet shall be accompanied by the song of the heart. Thy table is spread at first in the presence of thine enemies, and thy path of principle seems a path of sternness, but ere long law shall be lost in love, and thy cup shall overflow. Thy cup shall overflow in most abundance when thou thyself shalt overflow. Thou shalt find thy deepest peace when thou hast forgotten its presence in the care for interests not thine own, and thy new song shall reach its full melody when its joys shall be this: "Many shall see it, and fear, and shall trust in the Lord."

LXXXVIII.

THE PROMISE OF HEAVEN.

" Thy Spirit is good : lead me into the land of upright-
ness."—Ps. clxiii. 10.

How beautiful is this thought of the Psalmist !
There is a harmony, he says, between our
powers and our destiny. Goodness must lead
to the land of goodness. Is not this thought
of the Psalmist thy purest natural hope of
immortality ? Thou art conscious within thee
of great moral yearnings—yearnings which
this world cannot fill. Thou feelest in thy
heart aspirings which thy hand cannot reach,
ideals which thy life cannot realise, resolves
which thy will cannot execute. Are not these
aspirings the voice of the Spirit within thee ?
Yea, verily, and yet they are little more
than prophetic voices. How little hast thou
achieved of those aspirings even in thy best
moments, how little hast thou reached of those
ideals even in thy highest flights ! There is a
law in thy members warring against the law

of thy mind, and the weakness of thy flesh refuses to endorse the will of thy spirit. Is, then, the voice of God within thee a delusion? Nay, it is a prophecy. It reveals within thee more than thou canst embody without thee, but even so it predicts the advent of a higher power. Thy desire for goodness outruns thy capacity, yet it is the forerunner that tells that a larger capacity is coming. Is thy moral nature alone to be without its goal? Is everything to be provided for but thine aspirings after the beauty of holiness? Earth has filled all other capacities with employment and with enjoyment. This alone is unsatisfied here. Surely it shall be satisfied elsewhere, surely it shall be abundantly satisfied with the goodness of God's house and with the river of His pleasures. Everywhere but in thy heart there are heard already the full echoes of His praise, but within thy heart praise yet *waiteth* for Him. Thou art as yet only a promise to thy Maker, only a promise to thyself—a primrose in the cold, a dawn amid the shadows of the East. Yet the promise is made by something higher than thee—even the Spirit of

truth that is within thee. Thy spring demands
a summer, thy dawn is the pledge of a day.
The Spirit of God is good, therefore He shall
lead thee into the land of uprightness.

———

LXXXIX.

THE GLORY OF DIVINE LOVE.

*" The glory as of the only begotten of the Father, full of
grace and truth."*—JOHN i. 14.

To be full of grace and truth was indeed
a glory. It was the meeting of two things
which in the souls of men are antagonistic
to one another. There are souls which easily
bestow grace, which find it not hard to forgive, but they have often a dim perception
of the majesty of that truth which has been
violated. There are souls which have a clear
perception of the majesty of truth and a deep
sense of the sin that swerves from it, but they
are often inexorable in their justice and unable
to pardon; they have more truth than grace.

Here there is a perfect blending of extremes—
fulness of grace united to fulness of truth.
There is a forgiveness which is valueless
because there is no sense of wrong; there is a
sense of wrong which is forbidding because
there is no power of forgiveness. Here perfect
forgiveness is joined with perfect perception.
The glory of Christ's love is that it comes not
from darkness but from light ; He forgave the
sinner because He bore the sin. Never was
His forgiveness so complete as when He bore
His fullest witness to the awful truth. When
did He cry, "Father, forgive them: they know
not what they do"? Was it when He began
to think lightly of a violated law? Nay, it
was when the violated law was pressing upon
His soul, and the reproach of sin was breaking
His heart. His love was born of His pity, and
His pity was born of His purity. He felt
that we had already lost what He called our
souls. He saw us blind in a world of light,
deaf in a world of music, cold in a world of
warmth, heartless in a world of love, dead in
a world of life, and He lifted up His eyes and
cried: "Father, I am clouded in their darkness,

give them light; I am wounded in their sorrow, give them joy; I am pierced in their coldness, give them warmth; I am crucified in their death, give them life eternal." O Son of Man, that was Thine hour of glory. There, as in tints of blended rainbow, met colours that before had been disjoined—righteousness and peace, justice and forgiveness, penalty and pardon, the sentence of death and the message of life. Heaven and earth met together, judgment and mercy embraced each other in the fulness of Thy glory. The hour of sin's condemnation was the hour of a world's redemption. Grace and truth stood side by side.

XC.

STUBBORN SINS.

" Howbeit this kind goeth not out but by prayer and fasting."—MATT. xvii. 21.

THERE are temptations in the human soul which are not easily extinguished, which can only be extinguished through a process of pain. There are sins which may disappear in a moment, in the twinkling of an eye, at the blast of God's trump of judgment. Saul, who yesterday was walking in darkness, may see to-day a light above the brightness of the sun, and in an instant the old life may fall and a new life may rise. But Saul's temptation came from *within*, and was therefore sooner reached by the Spirit. There are temptations which come from without, which are given to the soul by its union with the body. These are they which ofttimes cast the man into the fire and ofttimes into the water; these are they which make him *lunatic* by destroying the force of his will. And these are they which go not out except by prayer and fasting. Prayer alone will not do; prayer gives but the grand resolution to abstain, but resolution, if not followed by action, fades in the light of morning. Fasting alone will not do; fasting is but the abstinence of the flesh, but the abstinence of the flesh is weariness without the consent of the spirit. The old habits of a man's life may not vanish in the moment of

his conversion. If thou hearest him confess
Christ to-day, and seest him act wrongfully
to-morrow, do not say that he was therefore
a hypocrite. "Did not I see thee in the
garden with Him?" is what thou shalt have to
ask of many, but do not thence conclude that
the garden was a delusion. The flowers that
are planted in Gethsemane rise slowly, and
they grow through struggle. There are dark
and rainy days, there are bleak and tempestuous nights, there are seasons of pro-
tracted cold which forbid the seed spon-
taneously to spring. Give thy charity to the
struggling soul. Give to its prayer and
fasting thy prayer and thy fasting. Forbear
to use thy full liberty until thy weak brother
also shall be free. Thou art able to go unhurt
through all the world, but thy brother cannot
yet go with thee; limit thyself for him, fast
for him. Thinkest thou that this is weakness? Hast thou not read of One who said,
not alone of His liberty but of His life, "I
have power to lay it down"? It is not weak
to be like Christ; it is strong—infinitely
strong. Thou *art* thy brother's keeper, let

P

Cain say as he will.   Thine is a Divine charge
—the charge of God, the charge of angels, the
charge of being a ministering spirit sent forth
to the heirs of salvation.   Keep that which
thy Father hath committed unto thee until
the liberation day.

XCI.

THE STRUGGLE SUCCEEDING LIGHT.

"*But call to remembrance the former days, in which, after
ye were illuminated, ye endured a great fight of afflictions.*"—HEB. x. 32.

"AFTER ye were illuminated."   Surely that
was a strange time for the birth of conflict.
I thought that the coming of light was the
signal for the *end* of war.   I thought that
when the heart was lighted up by the Spirit
of Christ, there must of necessity be a termina-
tion to all darkness.   Yes, but for that very
reason there must be a temporary experience
of pain—a pain which was foreign to the un-
regenerate heart.   It is a glorious thing to be

illuminated, but its first glory lies in this, that it shows me my past misery. When the Divine lamp is lighted in the room of my human nature, it lets me see how poorly that room is furnished. For the first time in my life I am pained with myself, I fight with myself. Before that time I was perfectly satisfied ; it was the satisfaction of ignorance. I did not see my poverty ; there was no light in the room. But now that the light has come, it has taken away my false rest; it has set me at war with myself; it has made me dissatisfied with my surroundings ; it has caused me to cry, "O wretched man that I am ! who shall deliver me from this body of death ?"

O Thou Spirit of light, I wait for Thee. I wait for Thee, knowing that when Thou comest Thou shalt come with a gift in Thy hand which the world would rather want— the gift of pain. I know that when Thy light shall rise within me the joy of the new vision shall be chequered by the sight of the old corruption. I know that when Thy power shall dawn within me there shall be stirred

within my heart the fires of a conflict to which
it now is stranger, for Thy new law in my
mind shall reveal the old law in my members.
But I would rather have Thy presence *with*
the pain than Thine absence without it.
Come into my heart with Thy Divine fire,
that all its base alloy may be purified. Pour
into my spirit Thy burning love, that I may
awake more and more to the sense of mine
own lovelessness. Breathe into my conscience
Thy quickening power, that I may feel more
and more the depth of mine own depravity.
Inspire into my soul the vision of Thy Divine
beauty, that I may learn more and more how
poor, how mean, how worthless is this natural
life of mine. I will begin the great struggle
when Thy light has come; I will fight the
fight of faith when Thy glory is risen upon
me.

XCII.

WHAT THE ANGELS STUDY.

"Which things the angels desire to look into."—
1 PET. i. 12.

WHAT were those things which were the sub-
jects of study to the angels? One would
think the meditations of the upper world
must be of a very transcendental nature, far
beyond our power of comprehension. In
truth these studies were not transcendental
at all; they were just the studies which
should be our own every day. We are told
in the preceding verse that there were two
things which the angels desired to look into—
"the sufferings of Christ" and the "glory
that should follow." What they wanted to
study beyond all other things was the road
by which ministration led to joy. Do you
wonder that this should have been a subject
of study to the angels? Does it seem to you
a theme too mean for angels? Have you forgotten what the angels are? Are they not all

ministering spirits, sent forth to minister unto them who shall be heirs of salvation? Why should not the ministering spirits study ministration, and study it in the person of Him who became the servant of all? Do we not all study those things which are most congruous to our nature? The poet is a student of poetry, the artist is a disciple of art. The angel was created to be a minister; wherefore should not he study *his* art? Why should not he go to the model Teacher in the art of ministering? Why should not he gaze even from the heights of heaven on the strait gate and the narrow way which led the Son of Man to the brow of Olivet? This would be sorrow, you say, and there can be no sorrow in heaven. Yes; but the thing which was sorrow on earth shall in heaven be turned into a joy. The selfish heart finds no joy in the study of ministration because it *is* selfish; let it become *un*selfish, let it be transmuted into the light of love, let it be lifted up to the heights of heaven, and that study will become its glory.

My soul, art thou prepared for the heavenly

meditation, the theme on which angels dwell?
If heaven came to thee to-night, would it
be to thee a joy? Is there within thee now
such a love for humanity as to make the care
of humanity a joyous subject of eternal study?
Is it with weariness and langour that thou
givest the thought of an hour to the problem
of human helpfulness? How, then, shalt thou
spend an eternity in which that problem
is the prevailing theme? Would not such
a heaven be to thee a land of inexpres-
sible pain? Prepare, then, to meet thy
God, O my soul. Thy God is love, and
He breathes the atmosphere of love. If
His atmosphere would be thy life and not
thy death, thou must be partaker of His
Spirit. Heaven is no home for the selfish;
they would not call it home. Wouldst thou
find in heaven a home, study on earth the
theme of the angels. Study the wants of
thy brother man, study the remedies for
human care, study the secret of successful
ministration, study, above all, that Divinely-
human sacrifice which teaches to all the ages
the glory of the Cross.

XCIII.

THE REASON FOR BURDEN-BEARING.

" Bear ye one another's burdens, for every man shall bear his own burden."—GAL. vi. 2, 5.

Is not this a strange reason given for burden-bearing?   We could have understood the sequence better if it had been said, "Bear ye one another's burdens, for it is not right that any man should bear his own;" but is it not strange to tell us, as a reason for bearing our brother's load, that "every man shall bear his own burden"?   No, it is not strange; it is sublimely, divinely beautiful.   What is the burden of which the apostle speaks?   It is the burden of temptation, the burden of being "overtaken in a fault."   What he wants to say is this: Bear ye one another's temptations, for ye have all temptations of your own for which you equally will need charity.   Thou that judgest thy brother, hast thou considered thyself?   Hast thou considered that thou also

hast a burden of temptation for which thy
brother will need to extend charity to *thee?*
Thine may not be the same burden as thy
brother's; thou mayest be strong in the place
wherein he is weak. But let not this be a
boast to thee; there is a place wherein thou
art weak and in which he is strong. When
thou ascendest the throne of judgment, and
when the books of thy brother's life are open
to thy view, remember that thou too hast
books to be opened. Remember that thou
too hast in the recesses of thy heart sins that
call for pardon, thoughts that await expiation,
deeds that require atonement, desires that cry
out to be purified; remember this, and thou
shalt bear with thy brother, and in thine hour
of need thy brother shall bear with thee.

My soul, wilt thou fulfil this royal law of
Christ? It is far in advance of the law of
Moses; the law of Moses said, "Thou shalt
not hurt," but this says, "Thou shalt bear."
It is not enough for thee not to injure thy
brother; thou must help him, thou must succour him, thou must do him good. Wouldst
thou be able to bear with his temptations?

then must thou be conscious of thine own. How shalt thou be conscious of thine own ? Come to the Dayspring from on high. Stand before the gaze of the searching purity, the spotless holiness, the stainless sinlessness of the Son of Man. There, in the vision of His humanity, thy humanity shall sink low and lie abased in the dust. There, in the blaze of His unblemished sunshine, thy flickering light shall be extinguished, and thou shalt learn thy darkness. The knowledge of thy darkness shall be thy first true light; it shall waken thy sympathy with man. When thou hast felt the pressure of thine own burdens, thou shalt lift the burden of thy brother; and in lifting the burden of thy brother thine own load shall fall.

XCIV.

THE CAUSE OF UNCHARITABLENESS.

*" But let every man prove his own work, and then shall .
he have rejoicing in himself alone, and not in
another."*—GAL. vi. 4.

PAUL says that the reason why men are
so uncharitable is that they do not know
themselves, do not prove their own work;
they think of themselves " more highly than
they ought to think." When we ask the
apostle how it is that a frail, sinful man can
believe himself to be pure, he answers, It is
because he compares his own badness with the
worse badness of others. That is what Paul
means by *rejoicing in another.* I have only
a small candle of virtue, quite unfit to guard
my footsteps, but then my brother has only a
taper. I go with my candle to his taper,
and I weigh that which is little in me against
that which is less in him. The comparison
enchants me; I come home rejoicing. I
feel myself a better man than I ever felt

before ; I magnify the light of my candle. But Paul says, This is only *rejoicing in another.* You are only comparing your badness with the more pronounced badness of your neighbour. Why not have an absolute standard ? why not prove your own work on its own merits, and have rejoicing in yourself alone ? You have brought your candle to the taper, and your heart is glad; why not bring it to the sunlight ? Why not carry it out into the blaze of day and weigh it against the majestic fulness of the light of heaven ? If your candle could stand that ordeal, then indeed you might have rejoicing in yourself alone, and no longer in the mere knowledge that another is worse than you.

My soul, thy light could not stand that ordeal. If thou shouldst bring thy candle into the blaze of day, it would have no glory by reason of the all-excelling glory. Wilt thou shrink from the ordeal that would prove thy nothingness ? thou art not wise in shrinking from it. What thou needest to make thee human is just the proof of thy nothingness, just the vision of thyself in thy poverty and in thy meanness. Go forth with thy candle into the light—the true Light that lighteth every man. Go forth into the presence, into the contact, of Him who is fairer than the children of men, the Chief among ten thousand, the altogether lovely. Go forth into the vision of that Sun of spotless righteousness that gathers no clouds upon His beams. In the hour when thou shalt behold Him thy candle shalt go out for evermore, and thou shalt be in darkness to thyself. O glorious darkness born of higher light, O grand humility sprung from a loftier ideal, O proud dissatisfaction telling of an enlarged capacity, my heart will not shrink from thee. I shall cease to rejoice in myself when I have come to rejoice in the perfect day.

XCV.

THE MEMORY OF THE HEART.

" His mother kept all these sayings in her heart."—
LUKE ii. 51.

THEY tell us that memory is one of the *in-tellectual* powers. I think that the strongest memory is a power of the heart. There are memories of the intellect which are short-lived and evanescent; they are like the morning cloud that vanishes away. But the things that are kept in the heart are not evanescent; they last for ever. There are those who complain of having short memories, but how often does it spring from want of sufficient interest? If we could transfer our duties from the intellect to the heart, we should rarely forget them. Love photographs the impressions of the past in colours that do not fade; the things which are kept in the heart are kept for ever.

My soul, cultivate the powers of thy heart. The heart has powers as well as the under-standing. Thou hast an eye of the heart

which sees deeper than the natural eye, which
is promised even the vision of God. Thou
hast au ear of the heart which hears more
keenly than the natural ear, which can catch
the Father's footsteps as He passes by. Thou
hast a judgment of the heart which can reason
more truly than the natural judgment, which
can penetrate the truth at a glance, and dis-
cern the end from the beginning. Thou hast
a memory of the heart which is longer than
the natural memory, which can preserve the
things of the far past in all the freshness of
yesterday, and keep in morning's glow the
remembrance of vanished days. Give to thy
God this memory of the heart. Remember
there is a connection between thy memory of
God and thy hope in God. What gives the
Psalmist such a golden view of the future
that he cries, "I shall not want"? It is just
his golden view of the past. He remembers
that God has already led him by the green
pastures and beside the still waters; that He
has already restored his very soul. What,
after that, can be too much to expect? What
makes the Apostle say that in the days to

come God will freely give him all things? It is just his memory that in the days gone by God had given him more than all things put together, had not withheld from him His only begotten Son. Thine is no irrational faith. Thy hope in rising suns comes from the memory of suns that have set; thy prospect is thy child of the retrospect; thy future is born of thy hitherto. Keep in thy heart all the steps of the old way. Remember the ram in the thicket that saved thee from sacrifice, the road across the sea that saved thee from storm, the manna in the wilderness that saved thee from famine, the tempering of Marah that saved thee from bitterness. Remember the mountains that were brought low, the doors that were opened, the crooked ways that became straight, and the rough places that were made plain. Remember, above all, that thy yesterday encloses a Divine sacrifice for thee, and thou wilt not be afraid of aught that to-morrow can bring; the prophecies of thy fear shall be conquered by the memories of thy heart.

XCVI.

HOW TO SHINE.

*" Ye are the light of the world. A city that is set on an hill
cannot be hid. Neither do men light a candle, and
put it under a bushel. . . . Let your light so shine
before men that they may see your good works, and
glorify your Father which is in heaven."*—MATT. V.
14-16.

OUR Lord is here teaching His disciples how to
shine. He tells them to avoid two extremes
—to beware on the one hand of affectation,
and on the other hand of want of *manifestation*. He says, in speaking of the first
extreme, that they need not be anxious to
display their light, " A city that is set on an
hill cannot be *hid*." He tells them that there
is a power within them which they could not
possibly conceal even if they were willing,
which would radiate from them in spite of
themselves, and reveal to the world the presence of something new. But, on the other
hand, He says that if they are to avoid
the extreme of a false display, they must

Q

equally avoid that of a false reticence. They are not to light a candle and put it under a bushel; they ought to place themselves in a situation advantageous for being seen, advantageous for influencing the mind of the world. How are these precepts of the Master to be reconciled? How are we to shine at once consciously and unconsciously—conscious of our power, and yet unconscious of our greatness? Our Lord tells us how. He says, "If you would shine effectively, if you would shine in such a way as to influence the minds of men, the motive of your shining must be a glory not your own." So shine that you may glorify another—"That men may see your good works, and glorify your Father which is in heaven." Let yours be the power of love, which is the power of dying, nay, of being already dead in the life of another. Forget your own glory in the glory of the Father, lose your own interest in the interest of the Father, merge your own will in the will of the Father. Let your brightest joy be to gladden Him, let your deepest grief be to pain Him, let your utmost effort be to serve Him.

Identify your pleasure with His profit, measure your loss by what men refuse to yield Him. And verily in that hour you *shall* shine—shine as the stars in the kingdom of your Father. The light on which you gaze shall pass through you, the love which is death shall be your rising, the forgetfulness which has buried self shall roll away the stone from the door of the sepulchre. Your true self shall live when your selfishness is dead, your personal being shall be powerful when you have forgot to seek for a personal joy. You shall shine as the planets of the night fed by the light of the reposing day, shine as the flowers of the field lit by the torch of morning. Men shall wonder at your power; you shall wonder most of all at your own power, for yours shall be the power that comes from humility, the power of souls that are crucified by love.

———

XCVII.

THE HEAVENLY IN THE EARTHLY.

"But we have this treasure in earthen vessels."—
2 Cor. iv. 7.

What treasure? The apostle tells us in the
preceding verse; it is "the light of the knowledge of the glory of God in the face of Jesus
Christ"—it is the treasure of Christian revelation. Why should this revelation be given in
earthen vessels? why, indeed, except that
thou to whom it is given art of the earth.
Would it be well for thee if thou couldst only
find Christ away from the earth, if the Divine
life could only be revealed to thee when thou
thyself wert withdrawn from earthly con-
cerns? Is it not a divinely beautiful thing
that Christ should meet thee in the world's
common things, that thou shouldst find the
heavenly treasure even in the earthly vessels?
Sometimes it has seemed to thee as if to find
the heavenly treasure thou wouldst need to

retire from the world, to·go away into some sequestered spot where the old pursuits and duties and avocations would exist no more. Yet in flying from the earthen vessels thou wouldst be flying from thy treasure.   It is not in thy freedom from earthly weakness, earthly contact, earthly struggle, that thou art nearest to the revelation of thy Lord ; no, my brother, it is *in* the weakness, *in* the struggle, *in* the contact with earthly things.   Art thou in the wilderness of temptation ? thou bearest, indeed, an earthen vessel, but it holds for thee a possible treasure of richest, purest gold; there, if thou wilt, thou canst meet the Spirit of Him who foiled the tempter and chose the narrow way.   Art thou in the midst of the great thoroughfare where toils the busy crowd, surrounded by its sins and jostled by its sorrows ? the vessel is, indeed, of earth, but the treasure is golden ; there, if thou wilt, thou canst meet the Spirit of Him who beheld the city and wept over it.   Art thou down in the valley of humiliation, bearing in thy heart the burden and the heat brought to thee by the world's day ? thine may there be the costliest of all treasures; for there, if thou wilt, thou canst meet the Spirit of Him who yielded up in Gethsemane His heart to a Father's will. Wouldst thou have a revelation of the cross? then must thou take up thine own cross—not an imaginary cross, not a sentimental cross, not a cross in the air, but the common earthen cross that falls to the lot of every man. Thou must take up the little petty cares of daily life, the trivial annoyances that are often worse to bear because they *are* trivial, the commonplace troubles that await every step of life's walk and every pressure of life's contact. Thou must take up, above all, thine own personal cross—that which men call thy weak point, and which thou wouldst gladly exchange for the cross of thy brother; thou must lift it and bear it manfully in the strength of the Son of Man. So shalt thou know Him; thine earthen vessel shall reveal to thee a treasure of revelation, and that which seemed to be the source of thine utmost weakness shall lead thee to the highest goal—the light of the knowledge of God.

XCVIII.

DEATH.

" The body without the spirit is dead."—JAS. ii. 26.

WHAT is death? Can any man define it? Does inspiration tell us what it is? Yes; in the words now before us we have the simplest, the shortest, the most explicit definition in the world; death is the body without the spirit. It is a wonderful explanation, marked off distinctly from all other explanations. It is not said that to die is to have the life of the body extinguished; no, the life is not extinguished, it is away; there is something absent, the body is *without* the spirit. It is not said that to die is to have the spirit without the body, in other words, that the spirit without the body is dead; no, the spirit cannot die, whether in the body or out of the body. Do not believe in the sleep of the soul; the soul never sleeps. Even in the watches of the night it is the body and not the soul that slumbers. The sleep of death is like the sleep of life; it belongs to the weary frame, not to the living spirit.

Thou who art weeping disconsolately over thy dead, there are words which have need to be uttered to thee, "He is not here, He is risen." Thou sayest, "He is dead," yet it is not so; death applies not to the spirit, and the spirit is the man. It is only the body that can die; it is the body without the spirit that is dead. Bethink thee, what mean these words, "Though He were dead, yet shall He live"? They mean that what thou callest death is not the contradiction of life. "I know that He shall rise again in the resurrection," says the weeping Martha at the grave of Bethany; yea, but, says the Master, thou expectest too little, for he that liveth and believeth in me shall never die at all. Martha thought that the life of the body was extinguished until that day when it should be revivified; she did not know that death was itself only the flight of the spirit. But thou shouldst know that, thou the child of resurrection, the recipient

of the dawn. Wherefore art thou hovering
ever near the spot where the dust reposes?
Why seekest thou the living among the dead?
Wherefore dost thou measure thy nearness to
the departed by thy nearness to the cemetery?
What communion has the cemetery with life,
what intercourse has the spirit with death?
If the departed should meet thee, it will not
be in the graveyard; it will be in those
moments when thou art furthest from the
graveyard. Not from out the tombstone shall
their voices come, but through the thoughts
that make thee forget the tombstone; not
from the symbols that are memories of death,
but through the hopes that tell of immortality.
In those moments in which heaven is opened
and the ladder is revealed stretching from earth
to sky; in those hours in which thine own spirit
is caught up to meet its Lord in the air; in
those days when from the top of Nebo faith
has beatific glimpses of the promised land; in
those seasons of summer warmth in which love
lifts up her voice and sings, "O death, where
is thy sting! O grave, where is thy victory!"
thou mayest picture, if thou wilt, the com-

munion of those ministering spirits sent forth
to minister unto them who shall be heirs of
salvation.

XCIX.

LIFE.

"*He that followeth me shall not walk in darkness, but
shall have the light of life.*"—JOHN viii. 12.

THERE is no light in the world so beautiful as
the light of life, nor is there any light so
revealing. The light of nature does not tell
us half so much that we would like to know.
There is a deeper revelation in the feeblest
breath of life than in all the tremors of all
the golden stars. The helpless cry of infancy
says more to the human soul than the sun
coming out of his chamber to run his race of
strength. The light of life carries in its
bosom all possible revelations; it reveals my
God and my immortality. All arguments for
my God grow pale before this certainty; all
arguments for my immortality faint in the
splendour of immortality begun. Life is the

Jacob's ladder that reaches from earth to heaven, that binds heaven to earth. The tiniest spark of life is the first step of an ascent whose midway is the angel, whose summit is the Throne of God. The more life is in me, the nearer I am to the Throne; my revelation grows not by what I get from without but by what I gain from within. If I had fulness of life I would have perfectness of vision; I would know what God is, what man is, what heaven is. Is it not written, "This is life eternal to know Thee"? And yet, marvellous to tell, this unspeakable glory may be mine—be mine now, here, in the midst of the present world: "He that followeth me shall not walk in darkness, but shall have the light of life." It is not by dying it shall come to me; it is by following—following the steps of the Master through life's strait gate and life's narrow way. It is by taking up the cross, by lifting the burden, by bearing the sacrifice, by doing the will, that the doctrine shall be known to me.

My soul, hast thou measured the true value of thy life? It lies not in its leading

Fulness of life

but in its following. It is not what thou
hast that reveals to thee thine immortality;
it is the sense of what thou hast not. The
measure of thee is thine aspiration—thy
thirst for Christ. All things rise to their
own level. If thy goal were the dust, thou
wouldst not seek to transcend the dust; thou
wouldst be satisfied. As long as thou art a
child of the dust thou *art* satisfied, and it is
the smallness of thy life that makes thee so.
But as thy life grows large it seeks more than
it can get below—the measure of the stature
of the perfect man, the fulness of Him that
filleth all in all. Thy glory is thy power to
follow; it tells thee there is something beyond
thee which yet is thy birthright. Thy cry for
God is the voice of God within thee, thy thirst
for the heavenly air is the breath of heaven
in thy heart. Thy conscious want is thine
open door, thy sense of sin is thy height of
Pisgah, and thy vision of the world's gathering shadow is made by the light of life
eternal.

a.

JESUS ONLY.

*" And when they had lifted up their eyes, they saw no
man, save Jesus only."*—MATT. xvii. 8.

IT is when I have lifted up mine eyes that I
am impressed with the solitary majesty of the
Son of Man; it is in the elevation of my own
moral view that I see Him to be what He is
—the King of kings. When my moral view
was not lofty I thought of Him as of other
men; I would have built for Moses and Elias
tabernacles by His side. But when the
transfiguration glory touched me I awoke to
His glory—His solitary, unrivalled glory.
I saw Him to be the chief among ten thousand, and fairer than the children of men.
Moses and Elias faded from the mountain's
brow, and *He* stood alone in peerless, un-
approachable splendour; I saw no man there
save Jesus only. I never knew before that it
was so great a thing to be good, for I had not

felt before the struggle between the old life and the new. It was only when, like the disciples on the mount, I had fallen prostrate in the struggle to be holy that I learned how really heroic it was to keep the conscience pure. It was from the depth of my conscious abasement that I lifted up mine eyes with longing to the hills of holiness. The Son of Man became to me more than all the sons of men—the first, the last, the only one, the altogether lovely. The strength of. Elias paled before Him. I felt that to conquer by fire was easier than to conquer by love, that to shed the blood of enemies required less strength than to shed one's own, and I lifted up mine eyes in reverence to behold Jesus only.

O Son of Man, may Thine image ever be thus peerless in my heart. May Thy presence fill all things, so as to leave no room for any other presence. May Thy glory be above the heavens, so that I have no need of the sun. May Thy tabernacle stretch for me over all creation, so that neither Moses nor Elias may build a tabernacle beside Thee. In all the forms of nature, in all the events of life, I would see Thee and Thee only. In all beauty I would behold the reflex of Thy beauty, in all wisdom I would see the inspiration of Thy wisdom, in all love I would trace the impress of Thy love. I would meet Thee in life's cloud alike as in its sunshine; I would feel that in Thy presence the night were even as the day. I would allow no tabernacle to be built beside Thee, in honour of chance or accident; my explanation of all things would be "The Lord reigneth." I would feel my *need* of Thy presence more and more. I know that the nearer I come to Thee the more will I experience the sensation of Thy disciple that I am "following afar off." But I will not shrink from that experience; it comes from the light that comes from Thee. I would be nearer to Thee every day, every hour, every moment, for it is only in being near to Thee that I shall learn how far off I am following Thee, how infinitely thou transcendest me. When I have beheld the summit of the mount I shall find none there but Thee.

CL.

THE GOODWILL OF THE BUSH.

" The goodwill of Him that dwelt in the bush."
—DEUT. xxxiii. 16.

Is not this a strange thing to place amongst the catalogue of human blessings? We can understand why Moses should have desired that his people might be blessed by God with " the precious things of heaven," with " the dew and the deep that coucheth beneath," with " the precious fruits brought forth by the sun and the precious things put forth by the moon." But why should he ask for them such a blessing as this?—the goodwill that God manifested when He dwelt in the unquenchable fire. Was not that aspect of Israel's God an aspect of deepest terror? did it not reveal Him in those attributes which do *not* suggest goodwill? Nay, my brother, it is not so. It is not only in the calm that the goodwill of thy God appears, it is not only in nature's

smile that the blessing of thy Father is seen.
The heart of thy Father beats for thee beneath
every cloud as well as in every sunbeam; the
blessing of thy Father is in thy night as well
as in thy day.   To thee, as to every man, He
comes betimes in a chariot of fire; with thee,
as with every man, He dwells betimes in the
burning bush of a wilderness; but the fire
chariot is *His* chariot, the burning bush is *His*
dwelling-place.   The fire of thy God is love;
its burning is the burning of love.   The pains
of thy life are not accidents; they are gifts
from thy Father's hand.   The fire of the
burning bush is meant to set fire to thy heart.
It is designed to kindle thee into a glow of
enthusiasm, to warm thee with the love of
humanity.   How *canst* thou be warmed with
the love of humanity if thou hast not in thee
that fellowship of the cross which unites soul
to soul.   The fire that comes to thee from
the bush is that which consumes the barrier between thy heart and the heart of thy
brother.   It destroys the middle wall of partition between you, and makes you one.   Before
the fire came to thee thou wert in the wilder-

ness alone ; thou hadst not felt the touch of nature that makes the world kin. But the fire opened the door of thy sympathy, and thy spirit passed through—passed into the heart, into the life of thy brother man to bear his burden and to carry his cross. There was no more solitude in thy wilderness ; to thee, as to Moses, the command came to enter into union with the afflictions of thy brethren. To thee, as to Moses, the mandate was given to go down into the valleys and join thyself to the sorrows of the sorrowing. It was to the ear of thy *sympathy* that mandate was addressed ; it came to thee through the fire. In the sense of thine own pain thou wert awakened to the universal pain ; in the bearing of thine own burden thou wert warmed into pity for all that bear. O blessed bush, whose burning in the wilderness has been my inspiration, I thank thee for my new life, my life of love. O Thou that still dwellest amid the fires of human suffering, and still knowest by sympathy the sorrows of Thy people, I bless Thee for Thy goodwill in the bush to me—that goodwill which, by sending me the mystery of pain, united me for evermore to the family of the sorrowful—to the heart of the Man of sorrows.

THE CARES OF GOD.

" He careth for you."—1 PET. v. 7.

THE old world looked upon Paradise as a place without care. It measured the majesty of the gods by their exemption from the cares of humanity. They dwelt on the top of Olympus, and rejoiced all the day in a sunshine whose cloudlessness was its carelessness—its absence of interest in the problems of human want, its recklessness of the fate of those who pine and suffer and die. But Christ opened the door of a new Paradise and let man see in. He gave to the human eye a totally different vision of the nature of Divine majesty. He showed that the majesty of God differed from the majesty of earthly kings not in having less, but in having more care. All earthly kinghood was defective by its inability to lift the whole burdens of a people; the government of the King of kings was supremely great because it could lift the burdens of all. That which distanced God from man was God's greater power of drawing near to the souls of man. Man held aloof from his brother man, and he had made his gods in his own image; Christ revealed a new image of God, a new thought of the Divine. Christ's majesty was the majesty of stooping; His cross was His crown. The sceptre which He wielded over humanity was the sceptre of love; because He was chief of all, He became the minister of all, because He was the ruler of all life, He gave His life a ransom for many.

My soul, hast thou emancipated thyself from that old epicurean dream?—the dream that thy greatness lies in thine independence. Is there nothing left in thee of that pagan ideal of a hero which tells men it is manly to be self-sufficient? Is there within thee still somewhat of the recklessness of that man who said: "Am I my brother's keeper?" Thinkest

thou that it is the badge of manliness to
say, " I do not care ? " It is not the badge of
manliness ; it is the mark of a child. Nothing
can be manliness which is not godliness, and
godliness is the presence of infinite care.
Wouldst thou be like God? it is well, but
thou wilt not reach thy goal in the manner of
the first Adam in the garden. Adam wanted
to know the difference of good and evil for the
pride of it ; he never thought of the care of it.
He did not know that it is just this knowledge
which constitutes the Divine burden—the longing for man's salvation. Wouldst thou be like
God? then thou must cease to be self-sufficient ;
thou must awake to the care for other souls ;
thou must learn what is meant when it is
said, "God is love." Love is joy—infinite
joy, but it is not epicurean joy. It is not the
joy of selfishness, but the joy of self-forgetfulness. The gladness of thy God is the gladness
of him who bears the harvest home, the gladness that carries in its bosom the spoils conquered from the field of sin, " This my son
was dead and is alive again, was lost and is
found." Wouldst thou reach the height of

the human, wouldst thou attain the image of
the Divine? enter thou into the joy of thy
Lord.

CIII.

THE BLASTS OF ADVERSITY.

*"Awake, O north wind; and come, thou south; blow
upon my garden, that the spices thereof may flow
out."*—SONG OF SOL. iv. 16.

THE spices in the garden of life only flow out
when the winds blow.   There are rich treasures
hidden in many souls which would remain
hidden for ever if the blast of adversity did
not disclose them.   There is more power in
every one of us than we ourselves know.
There is no depth we have explored so little
as the depth of our own heart.   There are latent
in our hearts vast susceptibilities, boundless
aspirations, intense powers of loving and of
working; but we ourselves are ignorant of
their presence until the winds blow.   We wait
for the breath of heaven to disengage the per-

fume that lies imprisoned in our flower of
life ; we need the north wind and the south to
blow upon our garden that the spices thereof
may flow out.

My soul, art thou afraid of the north and
the south winds ?   Art thou bemoaning the
hard Providence that has sent them into thy
garden ? Dost thou fear that they will destroy
the precious fruits of thy life ?   They are sent
into thy garden only that they may perfect
these fruits.   Does it seem to thee that the
Spirit of thy God hath departed from thee
because the north and the south winds have
begun to blow ? Nay, but the blowing of these
winds is itself the breath of the Spirit.   Hast
thou considered the life of Joseph as an ideal
type of the Providence that develops all life ?
Joseph, the shepherd boy, had a beauty of his
own, but it was not yet the highest beauty.
His soul was a fair garden, a potential garden
of the Lord, but it was not yet His actual
garden.   The seed was there of the future
fruits and flowers, but neither the fruits nor
the flowers had become visible.   Joseph's
beauty had not begun to diffuse itself.   His

was a life of dreams—beautiful, sentimental dreams, such as youth loves to cherish, but which as long as they are cherished prevent youth from being useful. And so the north wind and the south wind had to blow. The spices of that fair garden had to be released, and the winds of adversity came to release them. The dreaming boy had to be awakened from his dream, had to be taught that life is no dream. He had to be roused into the sense of human suffering, into a perception of the yoke of humanity, and he learned it by his own yoke—by the iron that entered into his soul. His last state was more glorious than his first because it was more out-flowing; his dreams about himself passed into his acts for others, and the sweet spices that had been concealed regaled the surrounding air. Even so, my soul, shall it be with thee when the north and the south winds shall blow.

CIV.

THE DISINTERESTEDNESS OF GOD'S CHOICE.

" I have chosen thee in the furnace of affliction."—
ISA. xlviii. 10.

IT is not in the furnace of affliction that man
commonly chooses man. Our friendships are
most frequently the fruit of summer days.
We cling often to the friend who is downtrodden, but our first love came to him when
he was not downtrodden; we did not *choose*
him in affliction. All the more marvellous,
therefore, is the Divine love. It is not merely
said that having loved us from the beginning
God loves us to the end, whatever may befall
us. This we should have expected from an
infinite love, it would not surprise us. But
here is a love which does not merely *endure*
in spite of the destitution of its object, but
which actually chooses its object in the
moment of its destitution. Here is a love
which comes to me not for what I have but

for what I have not, comes to me when I am wretched and miserable, and poor and blind and helpless, comes to me when I have nothing to give and nothing to attract.   It seeks me in my poverty that it may dower me with its wealth, it seeks me in my loneliness that it may glad me with its fellowship, it seeks me in my weariness that it may inspire me with its strength, it seeks me in my deformity that it may crown me with its beauty; it chooses me in my furnace of affliction.

O Thou Divine Love that passest the power of all human love to comprehend Thee, what shall I render unto Thee for Thine unspeakable gift—the gift of Thyself?   How shall I sufficiently bless Thee that Thou hast bent so low as to take cognisance of my lowliness. How shall I adequately praise Thee that Thou hast descended so deep as to come into contact with the depth of my meanness.   The most infinite thing about Thee to me is the infiniteness of Thy stooping; it is in Thy boundless power to bend that Thou surpassest the loves of men.   I accept Thy glorious offer of union with my nothingness.   I come to

Thee just as I am, as Thou hast chosen me   I
seek Thee without waiting for the ornaments of
life, knowing that when Thou shalt receive me
Thou shalt deck me with the gems of heaven
and adorn me with the jewels of Thy crown.
Out of the furnace of my affliction I fly to
Thee.

CV.

ISAAC.

*" And Isaac went out to meditate in the field at the
eventide."*—GEN. xxiv. 63.

WHAT a contrast there is between the life of
Abraham and the life of Isaac! The one is all
storm, the other is all calm. In the life of
Abraham we stand on the shore of a mighty
sea, whose bosom is ever ruffled, whose waves
are ever rolling ; in the life of Isaac we stand
by the rippling of a gentle stream, where there
are no storms to ruffle and no waves to roll.
Abraham is the man of action, and he is in-
creasingly the man of action ; his work grows

more pressing as he grows old.   But Isaac, even from manhood's dawn, is the man of meditation.   His is one of those introverted lives of which there is little to tell.   There is little to tell, not because the life is uneventful, but because the events are not seen; they lie not on the surface of history, they are transacted in the depths of the heart.   Think not that Isaac's calm was the calm of inanity; it was the calm of conquered storm.   Canst thou forget that if his was a placid manhood, it was because his had been a tempestuous youth. Some men get their cross in middle life, amid the burden and heat of the day; Isaac got his cross in the morning.   The fiery trial which one day comes to all of us, came to him on the threshold of life's door, and at the very moment when the bow of promise was seen in the sky, the blackness of darkness threatened to extinguish it for ever.   Was not the rest of his later years well earned?   Was it not fitting that he who at morning's dawn had climbed the sacrificial heights of Moriah, should be permitted, even in the blaze of noonday, to have something of the evening calm?

My soul, God has a time for thee to work and a time for thee to meditate. Would it not be well for thee to come up betimes into the secret place and rest awhile? The burden and heat of the day are hard to bear, and impossible to bear without the strength of the Spirit. Thinkest thou that the meditation of Isaac is a disqualifying for the work of Abraham? nay, it is a preparation for that work. Thou art called to go down into the valley, to lift the burdens of the laden, and to help the toil of the labouring. Would it not be well for thee to go up first into the mount of meditation, and get transfigured there? Would it not help thy coming work in the valley, if thou wert first to ascend into the elevation of aspiring prayer, where thou wouldst catch something of the radiance of thy Lord, and receive something of His glistening glory? Thy radiance on the mountain would not impede thy work in the valley; it would inspire it, it would strengthen it, it would ennoble it. Thou wouldst carry down with thee such a glittering of the transfiguration light, that the men at the foot of the mountain would take knowledge that thou hadst been with Jesus. There would go out from thee a marvellous virtue, a miraculous power, a supernatural energy, which everywhere would arrest and transform. Thou wouldst be animated by a new enthusiasm, impelled by a new force, driven on irresistibly by the impulse of light within. Arise, then, into thy mountain, O my soul. Take the wings of the morning, and ascend to meet thy Lord in the air. Enter for one blessed hour into the secret of His pavilion, and He will send thee a flash of light that will keep thee all the day. Thy work for man shall be glorious when thou hast meditated on the mount of God.

CVL.

CHRISTIAN PROMOTION.

" *Friend, go up higher.*"—Luke xiv. 10.

THERE are some of us who never get beyond the first step of Jacob's ladder. In taking that step we make the transition from death into life; but we are content with *mere* life— the life of an infant's breath. We are always talking of what we have been saved from in the *past*, we are always exulting in our liberation from the state which lies behind us. It is indeed beautiful to be grateful for the breath of existence, but have we considered what the breath of existence means? It means the introduction to boundless possibilities. Art thou exulting that thou hast placed thy foot on the first step of the ascending ladder? It is well, but let not this be thy resting-place. Remember it is after all only the first step, and it is the introduction to all the others. Thou standest between two worlds; below thee is the world of infinite death, above thee is the world of infinite life. It is good to look back upon the world of infinite death, to remember the depth out of which thou wert taken. But it is not good to be limited to that view. Thou art only on the first step, and there are myriads to come. Above thee there are heights of infinite progress waiting to be scaled, and from the summit of the sacred ladder a Divine voice descends into thine ear, "Friend, come up higher." Thou hast been dwelling with rapture on the thought of thy pardon, and truly it is a thought worthy of thy rapture. But there are greater raptures still before thee which thou must not neglect. Wilt thou be satisfied with mere pardon? If so, thine aspiration is smaller than it needs to be. Thou art a child of God, a son of the Highest, and thou hast a right to boundless expectations. Thou hast the promise of infinitude; wilt thou be satisfied with the finite? It is not enough for thee that God should pardon thee; He must fill thee with His own life. It is not enough for thee that thou shouldst escape the fires of hell; thou must aspire to enter into the blaze of the burning purity. It is not enough for thee that there is no longer any condemnation; thou must press towards the mark of a prize that is still beyond thee—the union and communion with God. Thou thinkest too meanly of thy destiny. Thou hast been freed from the fear of the famine in the far country, but thou art still content to be only a hired servant in thy

Father's house. Thou must yet arise and go
to thy Father and ask Him for something
more. There are gifts unspeakable which
still await thee—the ring, and the robe,
and the universal joy, for the voice of thy
Father is calling unto thee, "Friend, come
up higher.'

CVII.

RELIGIOUS ATTRACTIVENESS.

" *Let the beauty of the Lord our God be upon us.*"
—Ps. xc. 17.

THERE is a moral power in beauty; it elevates
the heart of the man that sees it. It is not
enough that a man should display the *law* of
holiness; he must display the beauty of holiness. There are some whose religion has
every quality but one—attractiveness. They
are animated by the sincerest motives, they
are ruled by the tenderest conscience, they are
influenced by the purest desires, yet their reli-

s

gion is withal a weapon in the hand, **not a magnet in the heart; it drives, but it does not draw.** They are impressed above all things with the power of the Lord, and they would like to display His power; they do not see that the uppermost garment of the religious life must be the *beauty* of the Lord. They have not measured the force of these words, "I, if I be lifted up from the earth, will *draw* all men unto me." The highest power of the cross is its attractiveness, its ability to allure, its beauty. Do not **think that the glory of** religion lies in the **number of things it can** *repel;* it lies in the number of things it can attract. The beauty of the Lord is an universally diffused beauty; there is no sphere which it refuses to animate. Hast thou not seen it in the world of nature how it pervades alike the highest and the lowliest? Thou beholdest it on the mountain-tops, and thou meetest it in the valleys. Thou seest it in the bespangled heavens, and thou tracest it in the colours of the earth. Thou findest it lighting up the wilderness and the solitary place, and thou discoverest it gilding the streets where pours the busy crowd, illuminating dusky lane and shady alley, kindling into a glow the common haunts of toilworn men. Truly it is beautifully said of the light of God's outward beauty, "There is nothing hid from the heat thereof."

O Thou who art the source of beauty, let Thy beauty overshadow my soul. Let Thy beauty be upon me as an outermost robe; *above* all, on the top of all, may I put on Thy charity. Help me to wear unsoiled everywhere the garment of Thy righteousness. Where Thou goest may I be able to go, where Thou dwellest may I be fit to dwell. May I go with Thee to the marriage feast without contamination; may I enter with Thee into the house of mourning without despair. May I stand with Thee in the streets of the great city where men strive and toil; may I commune with Thee in the solitary fields, where the lilies toil not nor spin. In the power of Thy Divine beauty may I be able to lift up things which are not beautiful; give me Thy strength to touch what the world could not touch without

stain. Help me to come into unharmed contact with that which would dim the impure
heart. Help me to take by the hand the
lepers, the demoniacs, the outcasts of the
world. Help me to give Thy beauty to
those that sit in ashes, Thy joy to those that
are in mourning, Thy garment of praise to
those that have the spirit of heaviness. Then
shall even the Gentiles come to Thy light,
and the powers of the world to the brightness of Thy rising. They shall see the King
no longer in His kingliness alone but in His
beauty. They were repelled by the fires of
Sinai, but they shall be attracted by the
lovelit peaks of Olivet; they have fled from
that gate of the house of God which is
guarded by the flaming sword, but they shall
return to enter it again by the gate of the
temple called Beautiful.

CVIII.

SPIRITUAL FEARLESSNESS.

"*For then shalt thou have thy delight in the Almighty, and shalt lift up thy face unto God.*"—JOB xxii. 26.

To lift up the face unto God is a beautiful image; it is the symbol of perfect confidence. We say in common language, when we wish to describe a man of bad conscience, that he cannot look us in the face. Such is in substance the thought here revealed. It is suggested that the bad conscience keeps the head downward towards the earth, prevents the man from gazing up even in his acts of prayer into the face of his Father. There is something sublimely beautiful in these words of the Master where He says of little children, "Their angels do always behold the *face* of my Father which is in heaven." It is the expression of fearless confidence. In Eastern lands it was only the few who were allowed to *stand* in the presence of the king, to gaze into the *face* of royalty. In the presence of the King of kings it is the little children that stand, it is the spirit of childhood that lifts up its face to God. There is no crouching, there is no timidity, there is no covering of the eyes in an attitude of servile fear; there is that beautiful boldness before the throne of the Heavenly grace which the childlike heart alone can feel; there is the lifting up of the eyes to God.

My soul, hast thou reached this glorious attitude of the childlike heart? hast thou attained to that perfect love which casteth out fear? Has thy religion become to thee anything more than a task, an ordeal, a daily and nightly penance which must somehow be got through, and which thou beginnest for the sake of getting through? Hast thou never risen from thine ashes in thy moments of prayer? have thy prayers never taken any form but that of abject servility? Hast thou never yet known what is meant by the joy of communion, the rapture of fellowship with God? Thou knowest what it is to be in *awe* of the

Almighty, but to have thy *delight* in the Almighty—hast thou realised that? Yet it is that and nothing less than that that is thy birthright; for this cause wast thou born, and to this end camest thou into the world, that thou mightst have communion with thy God. From thee there is desired no servile homage, only that homage of the heart whose name is love and whose nature is perfect freedom. It is thy heart and not thy life which thy Father would lead captive. He would enchain thee by the most golden of all chains—devotion to Himself; He would sway thee by the softest of all sceptres—the power of His love. Why art thou so fearful, O thou of little faith? Is it thy poverty that makes thee tremble? sayest thou that thou hast nothing of thine own to give? Neither have the waters of that sea when they look up by night at the form of the over-hanging moon; they have nothing of their own to give her, but they restore to her again the image she imprinted on their bosom. So shall it be with thee. Thy Father overhangs thee, broods over thee, calls to thee in a thousand voices, "Let there be light;" when thou shalt lift up thy face to Him, He shall see His image in thy bosom.

THE END.

CPSIA information can be obtained
at www.ICGtesting.com
Printed in the USA
LVHW082142300121
677928LV00006B/35

9 781340 563806